ST. FRANCIS DE SALES

ST. FRANCIS DE SALES

By

DR. MICHAEL MÜLLER

(PROFESSOR AT THE PHILOSOPHICAL AND
THEOLOGICAL UNIVERSITY OF BAMBERG)

LONDON
SHEED & WARD
MCMXXXVI

A TRANSLATION OF
" FROHE GOTTESLIEBE "
(COPYRIGHT : HERDER AND CO.
FREIBURG IM BREISGAU)

NIHIL OBSTAT : R. O. CAROLUS COLLINS, S.J.
CENSOR DEPUTATUS
IMPRIMATUR : CAN. S. BANFI
VIC. GEN.
SOUTHWARCI, 28 NOVEMBRIS 1936

PRINTED IN GREAT BRITAIN
BY THE WHITEFRIARS PRESS LTD.
LONDON AND TONBRIDGE
FOR SHEED AND WARD
31 PATERNOSTER ROW
LONDON, E.C.4

PREFACE

It was St. Thomas Aquinas who first systematised Catholic Moral Philosophy under two headings : first, so-called general Moral Theology in which he propounds principles ; and second, special Moral Theology in which he applies these principles to particular questions of life. This division has been preserved throughout the centuries, and in the doctrine of St. Francis de Sales it is very marked. There are first the basic principles on which the saint builds, and then the construction of a form of life based on these principles. Following St. Thomas, I intend in this book to show first the main principles of the Salesian ideal, and then to sketch the particular aspects of a life based on this ideal.

I am embarking on the task as a moral theologian. Recently there have been repeated attempts to define Moral Theology as a doctrine of sin, and Ascetic Theology as a doctrine of virtue. This definition is false, for, according to the Christian conception, evil is not an independent entity but only the negation of good. To affirm the opposite would be to relapse into a Gnostic dualism. The essential task of Catholic Moral Theology is to set forward the moral good and the virtuous ; and the doctrine of sin and vice is inseparable from this, being, as it is, the reverse side of human life. On the other hand, the aim of Ascetic Theology, as the expression itself implies, is to propound the particular practices which can help us to realise the ideal of conscience as it is laid

down by Moral Theology. Thus for the Christian, Moral
Theology is the supreme science of values, whereas
Ascetic Theology is a science of the means subordinate
to it and connected with it.

I hold that one aim of Catholic Moral Theology is
to set forth the positive side of Christian ethics. And this
brings us directly to the life doctrines of our saint and
doctor of the Church. In St. Francis we see the fundamental principle of Catholic morality—the love of God
conceived as the sun which shines over all Ascetic
Theology and ethics. In him we see, developed more
highly than almost anywhere else, the completeness and
unity of the whole way of life towards this final and
supreme principle. The scientific investigation of his
method means, therefore, an enrichment of Catholic
Moral Theology ; understanding his conception of the
world means opening a temple door to the learned, in
which the soul may find what it has been looking for so long.

My purpose, in embarking on this study, is to be of
service both to knowledge and to life. Unquestionably,
we are in possession of a scientific literature which is
outstanding both in quality and quantity, but which
neither seeks nor has any influence over ordinary life.
We have, also, a vast collection of edifying books for the
masses, but these are not scientific nor of a very high
spiritual standard. In this book I am trying to combine
both these types of literature. I am going to use a
scientific method of investigation which means going back
to the original sources, and then by a number of historical
and ideological sketches, I shall put the doctrine of St.
Francis de Sales in its proper place in the historic development of Catholic Moral and Ascetic Theology. For my
study of St. Francis de Sales and of theological literature

throughout the ages, I have thoroughly consulted all the best editions, and for the writings of St. Francis I have gone to the excellent *Annecy* edition which is the only really dependable one. I have been content with translations only when dealing with ascetical literature, especially the Spanish, as the original texts were not at my disposal. A glance through the works in question, however, satisfied me that my quotations, if not literally translated, gave the correct sense.

I have tried to present the fruits of my study in a form which will be understandable to all educated readers, and thus will be useful in everyday Catholic life. To-day the cry for religious renewal is louder than ever. History shows us two ways in which we can achieve this renewal.—from below, and from above. For the religious education of more simple people a large number of books is available. The more informed keep off them, for the most part ; they censure them for their insipidity and for their crude method of exposition. Of books for informed Catholics there is certainly no superfluity. And yet religious renewal should come from the intellectual class to the masses. That is the way which is of especial importance to-day.

I started on my work with all these considerations before me. My intention was to outline the conclusions I came to after a few public lectures. The number of my listeners —men and women of all classes—and the extent of their enthusiasm for the ideal of St. Francis, increased from lecture to lecture. May the influence of this book be for the greater honour of God, in Whose honour it was written.

MICHAEL MÜLLER.

BAMBERG, *June* 19*th*, 1933.

PUBLISHER'S NOTE

The Edition of the works of St. Francis de Sales which has been used is the one published at Annecy, the only complete one :

Œuvres de St. François de Sales, évêque et prince de Genève et docteur de l'Église. Edition complète d'après les autographes et les éditions originales . . . publiée . . . par les soins des religieuses de la Visitation du 1er monastère d'Annecy. Annecy. 1890.

This is quoted in the footnotes as the *Œuvres.*

CONTENTS

PART III

LOVE OF GOD AS CENTRE OF LIFE

PART IV

LOVE AND ASCETICISM

ST. FRANCIS DE SALES

INTRODUCTION TO THE LIFE AND WORK OF ST. FRANCIS DE SALES

A BRIEF survey of the honour paid to saints throughout the ages shows that preference has always been given to the saints who solved the specific religious problems of their own time. Thus the early Church honoured the martyrs, and the days of religious strife honoured the confessors. And when the external peace and welfare of the Church enabled its members to relapse into luxury and sensuality, it was the saints who renounced earthly possessions and dedicated themselves to the sanctification of their souls by becoming monks and hermits who were most esteemed. And now, in our own time, the universal honour paid to Theresa of the Child Jesus is a reaction against the complications of modern life, and against the dangerous tendency to admire a mere façade which has unfortunately penetrated even into religious culture. It is because of this that saints, to use the words of Alexander VIII, are always " the light of the Light who said : I am the Light of the World ". But they are also, according to Benedict XIV, *nova exempla virtutum*, always new and up-to-date examples of the religious life. Through the attitude taken to the particular circumstances and exigencies of the time, the soul of a saint receives new, unique and peculiar characteristics while always being the reflection of the external light.

St. Francis de Sales was for his own time and for the
whole of the modern epoch what the martyrs and confessors were to primitive Christianity. In the course of
the Sixteenth Century, a wave of pagan and heretical
thought inundated the Christian peoples and clashed
with a counter-wave of mystical and exaggeratedly
ascetical thought. The conflict between the natural and
the supernatural, between life in the world and the desire
to get to heaven, was as marked then as it is to-day. A
number of Catholic writers imagined that they could deal
with the problem by completely submerging the natural
side of life. But the inadequacy of this method was
evident. The killing of life, as given by nature and therefore willed by God, the resultant spiritual emigration, the
secessio plebis in montem sacrum, has never been able to solve
the question in a real way, for it has never mastered
reality—any more then than now. The point was to
formulate a new ideal that integrated earthly culture and
deep Christianity, that harmonised Humanism with
Catholicism, that blended one's duties on earth with
surrender to God, and enabled one to be a true man and
at the same time become a saint. The necessity of the
synthesis had been recognised for a long time. People
were fully aware of it by the end of the Sixteenth Century.
But the capability of attaining it was lacking. For this
great work it was necessary to have the combined strength
of a religious genius, a saint and an educated man of the
world. This "gentleman saint" was St. Francis de
Sales.

*   *   *   *   *

On Thursday evening, August 21st, 1567, there was
intense excitement in the castle of the family de Sales,
near Thorens, about thirty miles south of Geneva. The

heir of the prince had been born. He had been longed
for ardently and he had now arrived two months earlier
than was expected. His father was in the middle forties
and his mother had not yet reached the age of fifteen.
The tiny Françoise de Siennaz had been given in marriage
at the age of seven. And seven years later she held her
first-born child in her arms. The boy was very " small
and delicate ",[1] and the child-mother had not yet grown
up to her task. But finally the child throve.

Thus the life of the great St. Francis de Sales began in
circumstances in no way favourable. The belief held by
so many people that the saints walk on rose-leaves from
their birth and that a kindly providence removes every
obstacle from their way is destroyed by this example
alone. When Francis was six, his father sent him to
school at La Roche so that he should get used to inter-
course with children of his own age. When he was ten
he received his first communion and was confirmed. At
the age of fourteen he went to Paris, accompanied by a
tutor, to receive a finishing-education at the college of the
Jesuits. According to the records of contemporaries, the
demands made by that school seem to have been rather
exorbitant. For example de Mesme relates that he learnt
the whole of the *Iliad* by heart in eighteen months ; and
Montaigne complains of the strict discipline. Francis
does not seem to have suffered from this, however ; at
least he tells us in 1615 that children had to learn much
more then than they did in his youth. In Paris he
studied the ancient languages—Latin, Greek and Hebrew
—philosophy " following the wish of his father " as he
said later, and theology " for his own satisfaction ". Also,

---

[1] Charles Auguste de Sales, *Histoire du bienheureux François de Sales* (Paris,
1857), pp. 1–2.

as befitted a young nobleman, he took lessons in dancing, riding and fencing. His father had sternly commanded him exercise in these accomplishments. He entered polite society circles, especially at the house of the Duke of Mercœur. And thus, effortlessly, he gained the sure, unruffled and polite bearing which is so difficult to acquire in later life. It was here, too, that he learnt the use of the fork which Henry III had introduced at court ; previously people had been content to use a knife and their fingers. In this association with the high aristocracy, Francis also obtained insight into the spirit and the problems of the age. He heard the discussions between the Catholics and the Huguenots and the severe criticism levelled against the court in the person of the King. Finally, he was present at the revolt of Paris. The doors of the school were shut. Henry III secretly left the city. And for Francis it was the end of his studies in Paris.

After a short stay at home, his father sent him to the famous University of Padua. The opulence of Venice had inspired the growth of this centre of cultural life. There were 20,000 students in the town, and there are many accounts of their tyranny and monopolising of it. At this time Francis was about twenty-three. Two episodes serve to show the disorderly life of the students and Francis's attitude towards it. The medical students once had a shortage of corpses for anatomy. Without a moment's hesitation they broke into the cemeteries, with the result that the inhabitants of the town guarded the graves of their loved ones with arms. The students, however, stole the corpses, using weapons themselves. At that time Francis was critically ill, and he commanded his tutor to " give up his corpse to the students of medicine and surgery " as soon as he was dead, so that at least in death he should serve the public good—a thing he had not yet accomplished in life.

Another event which equally shows the nature of his character is told by Charles Auguste de Sales, the nephew of Francis and his biographer. It seems that picking quarrels in the streets of Padua was no rare event with the students, and as the sword was swiftly drawn, people were often wounded and sometimes even killed. One evening a few students were spoiling for a quarrel, and they decided to expose the suspected cowardice of the " pious " nobleman, Francis. With weapons in hand they bore down on him, but Francis, instead of fleeing as they anticipated, drew his sword and fenced dexterously, finally forcing his aggressors to ask forgiveness. He had not been taught fencing in Paris in vain.

Thus the salient characteristics of the future saint are visible in the young man ; the frank acceptance of the necessities of life, the kind and friendly readiness to bridge human differences, the clear and courteous considerateness and manly courage. And for all his goodness, love and power of yielding, he knows how to draw his sword and repulse a man of force.

Francis studied jurisprudence in Padua—in this, as in Paris, obedient to his father's wish—and then theology, obedient to his own. His juridical studies ended in promotion. With youthful extravagance he said in his speech of thanksgiving that " the bestowal of the degree of doctor " is " the highest that can be realised in mortal life, because all other distinctions are due either to propitious fortune or physical advantages. The honour of the doctorate, however, is an adornment of virtue alone ". Then he praised the " sacred science of Law ", and finally compared the university to a " mountain

whose top, like a second Parnassus, is inhabited by the
nine muses ".[1]

Brought up since earliest childhood in the Christian
way of life by a pious mother and a strict father, and then
directed and educated by the Jesuits, his soul preserved
its innocent tenderness, and later gained a manly strength
and dignity as the result of his clashes with the loose
young students and nobility at the University. A few
rules of life which he drew up reveal his attitude. We
hear first of monthly, and then of weekly, communions
and of his careful preparation for them, and we get a
glimpse of his life of prayer and his method of contemplation. Even the mystical element in him which came to
life much later in the *Traitté* were apparent in the young
student. Every day he saved some free time so that his
soul could rest in peace with God, for, " just as the body
needs sleep so as to rest its weary limbs and refresh it, so
the soul needs a certain time to sleep and rest in the pure
arms of the heavenly bridegroom so that thereby the
fresh elasticity of spiritual capabilities may be restored ".
Francis considered this peace in God as so important that
he resolved to dedicate part of the night to it when it was
impossible to find " any other hour for this spiritual
repose ".

" I will do it this way. If it is nowise possible other
than in bed, either I will remain awake longer than the
others . . . or I will get up earlier than the others in
the morning to ponder the word of Our Lord : Watch
and pray so that ye fall not into temptation."

Francis regulated his social life with special care. He
decided to keep a reserve with regard to his relationships.
His maxim was : Friendly with all, intimate with only

[1] Ch. A. de Sales, *op. cit.*, p. 40.

a few. This was in no way an unnecessary precaution on his part. We hear that once he was presented to a harlot who was introduced to him as the wife of a famous lawyer. When he saw through the deception he said : " I thought I was with an honourable woman in a virtuous house ; I see that the house is a brothel and you a whore ".[1]

He never deviated from virtue. In his development there is no "conversion". His life is not cut into two parts—a period of sin and a period of virtuousness. Thus his spiritual make-up is free from that interior clash experienced by so many converts, which only too easily leads to an exaggerated rigour by way of reaction against the unfortunate experiences of youth. Nevertheless, Francis had sufficient upheavals as a youth to give his religious thought and experience a particular stamp of its own.

Calvin had preached an absolute predestination to heaven or hell. Theologians in Paris had debated the question passionately—the question as to whether God determined the eternal happiness or eternal damnation of men according to their future conduct in life or regardless of it. As an intelligent youth—he must have been about nineteen—Francis took a lively interest in this quarrel. This theoretical question became a personal life-question for him, and he asked himself whether he was predestined to salvation or damnation. Some sort of psychological depression, usual enough in adolescence, led him to answer in the unfortunate sense, and he condemned himself to hell. His natural desire for self-affirmation fought against such a terrible fate, though his piety, at the same time, urged submission to the supposed decree of the Almighty. A frightful struggle

[1] Œuvres, Vol. XXII, pp. 12, 28. Ch. A. de Sales, op. cit., p. 32.

ravaged his soul and six weeks were spent in agonising
torture. His physical strength broke down, and the
unbearable tension pressed all the more for some con-
clusive decision. From the psychological point of view
there were two solutions, either a sharp turn to the left—
enjoy this life seeing that the next is already lost ; or the
subduing of self-love by love of God. Francis's deep-
rooted piety selected the second way out. He acquiesced
in his damnation ; he was ready to go to hell if it was
pleasing to God. " Yea, Father, Thy will be done . . . "
But with this inhuman sacrifice the spell was broken.
Francis knelt before the picture of the black Madonna at
Saint-Etienne-des-Près and recited the *Memorare*. Then it
came over him like a wave of light that damnation was
really a very unworthy glorification of God. No, God
Who so loved the world that He gave His only-begotten
Son to die for it, did not intend us for hell but for heaven.
And so the frightful struggle ended in a triumphant
optimism ; and the end of the time of suffering was the
birthday of that joyous outlook on life which was inseparable from him thenceforward. From the theological
point of view, Francis had turned to Molinism. That
was the primary result of his experience. As a secondary
result came his ascetical exhortation to a complete
indifference to the values of this life—even to the extent
of resigning one's own salvation. Through this acute
tension which St. Francis himself calls an " impossible
state," he gained yet a third life-value : a deep understanding of the tormenting nights of the soul, and a deep
sympathy with them. Men acquire the gentleness with
which to heal suffering in others, only by the personal
experience of similar suffering.

In the new year, 1593, Francis, at the age of twenty-

five, returned home. His father had prepared all of the
best for his talented son—but, without knowing of his
son's secret yearning for the priesthood. A lavish law
library greeted the Doctor of Law ; a grant of property
made him lord of Villa Reget in his own right ; he had a
clear path to a lawyership in the supreme senate of
Chambéry ; a " very beautiful " and " really virtuous
maiden", the only daughter of one of the best and richest
families in the land, awaited him as his chosen fiancée.
Francis was not a little concerned by his father's kindness
and autocracy. He decided to pursue a policy of delay.
He went to Chambéry and was greeted with praise and
admiration ; with his father he paid the promised visit
to the family of his intended fiancée, but he was so cold
that the visit could not be treated as more than the
fulfilling of a polite duty. His father was angry at this
attempt of his son's to frustrate the plans which he had
devised so ably.

At this time Francis made a confidante of his mother
and of his cousin Louis who was a prebendary in Annecy.
Louis knew of Francis's theological education, and he
also knew how his ambitious father could be won over.
The provost of Annecy had just died. Louis obtained
from Rome the nomination of his cousin as Provost.
Francis, who had not the slightest idea of this plan, was
rather shocked ; he had wanted to be a priest, but he
had not aspired to a prelacy. But his cousin pointed
out to him that this move was the only way of con-
ciliating his father. Together they approached his father,
and Francis presented his petition. The canon came to
his assistance with the papal decree in his hand, and the
mother acted as mediator. In this way the victory was
won and Francis's father consented to seeing his son as a

provost instead of a senator. In June Francis received
minor orders, and on December 18th, 1593, he was
ordained a priest. In a letter to his friend Favre he
reveals the feelings with which he awaited his ordination.
The responsibilities which confronted him were very
great, but his trust in God was greater still. " Do not
believe," he writes, " that these holy mysteries fill my
soul with such alarm that there is no room for hope and
joy. . . . I am full of joy." [1]

Thus, at the age of twenty-six, Francis occupied a place
second only to the bishop. There was no lack of envy
and intrigue, but Francis showed that it had not been
his desire to have the dignity and comfort of a prelacy.
Chablais, a district on the southern side of the Lake of
Geneva, had once again come into the hands of the
Catholic Duke of Savoy who wished to bring back his
people to the faith which had been lost in favour of
Calvinism under the military force of Geneva and Berne.
He begged the bishop to send missionaries there. It was
a blatantly dangerous undertaking, for, with the flaming
confessional hatreds of the time, the prospect of a martyr's
crown seemed considerably greater than the prospect of
success. The bishop placed the matter before the clergy
to see if some of them would offer themselves voluntarily.
Francis volunteered. His father was furious and his
mother dissolved into tears. Nevertheless, in the middle
of September, 1594, he set out for the mission fields
accompanied by his cousin, Canon Louis, and carrying
nothing but a few books including the controversies of
Bellarmine. As residence, Francis was allotted the
unconquerable ducal stronghold of Allinges. From there
they were to embark on their activities, going daily rounds

[1] Œuvres, Vol. XI, p. 40.

and every night returning to the fortress, otherwise there was no guarantee for their lives. The result of the first winter's work was a pistol attack, frost-bite in the feet and only one conversion, if it could so be called—a lapsed Catholic who came back to the Church.

Thereupon Francis changed his method. The authorities had forbidden the Protestants to go to his sermons, and so Francis seized his pen and wrote leaflets. If people dared not listen to his word at least they would have the opportunity of reading what he had to say in their homes. It was from the collection of these leaflets that his book of *Controversies* was composed later. But all his trouble was vain. Sad, disillusioned, worn out, he wrote after six months of fruitless work : " This country is like a completely paralysed man. Before it is in a position to walk I shall easily be able to make a journey home. . . . Things become more difficult for me from day to day ".

Then at last came the first real result—the conversion of a lawyer on August 20th, 1595, and following on that several councillors began discussions with Francis. Francis, who always felt the need to express his feelings, wrote of this to his friend Favre : " And now, my brother, the gates have opened wide and joyfully to this Christian harvest. Yesterday M. d'Avully and the gentlemen of the council went almost openly to the sermon. On account of the ban they did not dare to come completely openly. . . . Now the thing is assured to me, for once they begin to discuss they will soon—as the proverb says—capitulate ". His hopes and also his missionary methods were fully justified by the results. A public disputation in Geneva strengthened his authority, though a visit to Beza, the leading Reformer in Geneva,

which Francis undertook at papal command, met with
no success. Nevertheless, the ice was broken in the
Chablais and the number of conversions increased from
month to month. Four years after the first discouraging
beginnings, the Duke and a Cardinal Legate from the
Pope arrived in Thonon to commemorate the fourfold
prayer with festive pageantry. The Duke introduced
Francis to the Cardinal as " the Apostle of the Chablais ".[1]

As the result of a commission from his bishop, Francis
went to Paris. His business was to deal with the religious
situation in the district of Gex, which ecclesiastically
belonged to the diocese of Anneçy but politically to
France. The negotiations were carried on by the court
in a long drawn-out way, and thus the saint had eight
months' opportunity to acquaint himself with French
Catholicism. It is equally important for us to become
acquainted with it for it is the key to understanding the
doctrine and writings of the saint.

At that time, as to-day, there was very little unity.
The majority of educated Catholics stood fast by their
beliefs, going to Sunday Mass, Lenten sermons and feast-
day processions—a state of affairs which the Huguenot
opposition had brought about. Yet where moral living
and personal thought and experience were concerned,
this religious conviction had very little influence and
" divine philosophy " was the criterion instead. And
this was not the Christian philosophy of Scholasticism
but the philosophy of ancient times which had been
awakened by Humanism. One followed, according to
one's preference, the wisdom of Epicurus or of the Stoa ;
or perhaps the man really skilled in the art of living
combined them both—and was Epicurean with regard to

[1] Œuvres, Vol. XI, pp. 268–270. Ch. A. de Sales, op. cit., pp. 137 sq.

pleasure and stoical with regard to pain. At the top reigned Henry IV—intelligent, lovable and, as is presumed, at that time a Catholic by conviction. But it was known that on the very day when His Majesty was married by proxy to Maria de Medicis in Florence, he appeared at table by the side of his mistress. He wanted a solid clergy and took pains in educating bishops for his kingdom and as soon as he got to know Francis de Sales he held him in high esteem. But at the same period he nominated a child of four as bishop, and thought that he would easily obtain absolution from this confessor. Thus to the people religion played almost the same part as service to a king. In service one did homage to His Majesty and, that being done, one retired into private life and amused oneself according to one's own whims and fancies.

Besides this group, which comprised the majority of the people, Francis also observed the few representatives of the opposite extreme—the followers of a mystical and cloisterish piety who, though living in the world, longed passionately for the cloister, and therefore, as Francis put it later, " always had their hearts in different places from their duty ". Only in one thing were the members of the groups united : they all suffered from an inner conflict between religion and life—a conflict which is only overcome by a true devotion that rules over the whole personality and the whole life.

Only a small circle of noble people had escaped both Scylla and Charybdis in undertaking the task of leading a deeply religious life in the midst of the world. Among these was Madame Acarie who presented herself to the world as pleasant, pretty, lovable, very elegantly dressed, yet very serene. This lady, Francis says, wore *décolleté* dresses in obedience to her husband without harming herself in any way. She appeared in society, in fact, quite overloaded with vanities and yet she was " one of the greatest souls "—a mystic, full of the grace of God, who had experienced ecstacies. Francis frequented her salon and there he made the acquaintance of the recognised leaders of religious life, the most spiritual priests and the best theologians of Paris. Madame Acarie opened her soul to him, and Francis gazed in wonder at its holiness in which he could scarcely discover a venial sin. He visited her " nearly every day " and nineteen years later, at the end of his life, he still gratefully remembered the stimulating effect that those " very holy confidences " had had on him.

One might well wonder why Madame Acarie did not become for him what, two years later, Madame de Chantal became—his " most beloved soul ", his second Ego. Madame Acarie had laid bare to him her " so holy and enlightened soul " and he had undertaken to be her confessor during his sojourn in Paris. Why did he not continue directing her ? Did he miss, perhaps, those qualities which he later designated as the necessary basis of friendship ? Possibly : or perhaps he discerned, in the circle of her spiritual directors and advisers, outlooks which conflicted with his own and methods with which he did not intend to comply. At least we know one thing : that he did not yet want to break his reserve ; he still wanted to confine himself to watching and learning. And it was precisely in this study of the forces that surrounded him that he became aware of his own ideal of devotion and direction of souls. He arrived in Paris as a famous and popular missionary ; he left it as the herald of a new ideal. When he was back in Anneçy he wrote his first letters of spiritual direction and he was fully conscious of the singularity of his method. About the Paris theologians he said in November, 1602 : " I admire their method but it is not mine ".[1]

On the journey home Francis received the news of the death of his bishop. He himself was, as coadjutor, designated to succeed him. On December 8th, 1602, in the village church where he had been baptised, he received consecration as a bishop.

His public activities were always prompted by a clear understanding of the weakness of the time and by a saviour's love for his flock. He held the reins with a strong hand. If discipline was ignored in town or monastery, he forced through reforms ; but he never forgot that though penalties can stem evil, only love can awaken new life. He was untiringly scrupulous in the carrying-out of the decrees of the Council of Trent. He traversed his diocese on horse-back—over the " land of glaciers ", the Mont Blanc district, upwards " from cliff to cliff "—to the most distant villages and the most solitary farms ; he was " never more than half a day in the same place ", and wherever he was he inquired into and tested the condition of the Church, as the Council of Trent had prescribed. He preached daily, " and often twice daily " and conferred on " a countless multitude " the sacrament of confirmation. He returned to Annecy sometimes after a week's, sometimes after a month's, journey, and was so physically exhausted that he was at times ill, but his soul was always full of joy. He had given himself wholly and entirely to his people and " how this good people . . . honoured its bishop . . . ! "

His fame as a preacher spread far and wide through this mountain homeland. He was invited to preach

[1] _Œuvres_, Vol. XII, p. 148.

Lenten sermons, and in Dijon, Chambéry, Grenoble and Paris people flocked to hear him. In the old cathedral at Annecy, however, he showed how he could " become a child with children ", and there was many a chirp of half-suppressed laughter rising to the pointed Gothic arches. Once the saint explained : " We were talking about masks and balls and I was in my good humour ". Of the sensitive fervour of the children themselves we get a glimpse in this remark made by one of them : " Jesus is more mine than I His ".

He gave especial care to the cultivation of knowledge. He was convinced that the Reformation had caused the harm it had simply because " we confined ourselves to saying our breviaries and did not think of acquiring scientific knowledge "—" knowledge is the priest's eighth sacrament ". He was therefore especially anxious that his theologians should be instructed in fundamentals and he sent his most gifted priests abroad, taking endless pains in obtaining their educational and material wherewithal. In the winter of 1608–9 he founded, in conjunction with his friend Favre, an academy in the little town of Annecy which was devoted especially to the teaching of literature.

For Francis's development the year 1604 had special significance. He was in his thirty-seventh year and he preached the Lenten sermons in Dijon in accordance with the request of the magistrate. It was here that he became acquainted with Madame de Chantal. She was thirty years old at that time and already a widow of three years' standing ; she lived with her four children in the house of her father who was president of the Dijon parliament. Religious from childhood, after her husband's death she had dedicated herself entirely to a life of devotion. But she had an over-exaggerated mystical tendency and contemplated shutting herself off from the world as the sole and unique condition of a complete love of God. Thus she bewailed the fact that her duties to her four children prevented her entering a convent or fleeing to the Holy Land. At the same time her spiritual director was a man whose lack of understanding, while humbling her, never gave her restless soul any chance of inner peace. She saw and heard the famous Bishop of Geneva in her father's house, in the company of her brother who had been Archbishop of Bourges, and in the pulpit. Such a flow of restful and happy spirituality emanated from his being that it awakened her afflicted soul to new hope, new inspiration and a new desire to do great things. Francis appeared to her " like an angel of the Lord " and, as she said later, she admired everything he said and did. " From the very beginning and from the depths of my heart, I called him a saint." Francis himself regarded the Baroness with lively interest. He sought out her company and soon felt the close relationship of their souls. He realised that this woman had already partly achieved his ideal—the mingling of culture with deep devotion— and that she was well qualified to reach his ideal of perfection altogether. Then Francis abandoned the position of detached onlooker in which he had allowed what happened to happen, and in which he had built his outlook on life from the detached contemplation and criticism of what occurred around him. This change had begun with his departure from Paris ; and now, if his eye chanced on some material, he was filled with a desire to shape it. Thus the sight of the beautiful soul of Madame de Chantal inflamed his will to create. As an artist changes some line in a beautiful picture to make it more beautiful still, he began to improve her soul, unasked.

There was a strange contradiction between the simplicity of thought and the elaborateness of dress in Madame de Chantal ; so Francis asked her, " Are you contemplating re-marriage, Madame ? " She answered no. " Then you should remove the placard." Madame de Chantal understood and the next time they met she had doffed her finery.[1] On Wednesday of Passion Week she invited him to a conference. Later Francis himself told the Baroness what he had experienced while there : " From the first moment that you began to speak to me about your interior life, God gave me a great love for your soul ". And when he left Dijon, the separation meant no interruption of their friendship. On the evening of the first day's journey he sent a note to Madame de Chantal : " God has given me to you ; every hour it becomes more evident to me ".

That brief phrase reveals Francis's thoughts on that journey and indicates the chief content of his spiritual meditations throughout the following weeks. He was well aware that their souls had come into contact ; and his ability to lead and his gift of friendship were ready to develop. Yet he was so self-disciplined that he was unused to giving way to his own wishes, so now began that inner conflict which usually precedes great decisions. At the heart of the struggle lay the difficult problem of friendship between men and women. What was God's will ?—to renounce the incipient friendship or to carry it through and with it the direction of her soul ? If the former, Francis was ready ; if the latter, they would ascend the steep path to Heaven hand in hand. During his whole life, Francis never did anything in haste. Four months

[1] M. Fr. Mad. de Changy, *Mémoires sur la vie et les virtus de Ste. J. F. Fremyot de Chantal*, pp. 1, 11–13.

elapsed in the strictest self-examination and in supplication to God for clarity and truth. Neither the wish of the
Baroness nor his own inclination was to affect him—but
only God's will. At last he reached that height where all
earthly considerations fade : his own will was silent and
God alone was there in overwhelming force. Straightway
he summoned Madame de Chantal to St. Claude. On
the morning of August 25th, 1604, he informed her that
" It is really God's will that I should take over the direction
of your soul and that you should follow my counsel. Do not
wonder that I was so long in coming to this decision.
I wanted to be convinced as to where the will of God lay.
In such matters nothing should happen save by His hand."

And then from the lovingness of his heart Francis devised
the way in which to bind their souls together " for ever
and without any reservation ", through a love " whiter
than snow and purer than the sun ". The Baroness
made her confession and Francis undertook the direction
of her soul. Both the saints renewed their vow of eternal
chastity and during Mass they laid their hearts and
promises at the feet of God. The future showed that that
day at St. Claude was, for both the saints, what Francis
had hoped it would be : a source of strength for eternal
life, " *le jour fourrier du jour eternel* ". [1]

With unparalleled self-sacrifice, Francis dedicated the
finest activity of his life to the education of his friend's
soul, and proved the truth of Erasmus' dictum : " the
best way of learning is teaching ". In raising up a saint,
he himself became a saint ; in directing her soul, he
became a great director of all souls. In Madame de
Chantal he realised his ideal of sanctity ; she was the
incarnation of his ideal and thus she stimulated his spirit

[1] *Œuvres*, Vol. XII, pp. 353, 367.

to efforts always new—as a lovely model inspires an artist to further effort and further development. Meanwhile a group of religious people, scattered through Savoy and France, gathered around him in spirit and he wrote them numerous letters which frequently became short tracts and were circulated among his followers.

The young Madame de Charmoisy, " a perfect and accomplished lady with a heart of gold ", as Francis described her, showed these writings to Fr. Jean Fourier, the rector of the Jesuit College at Chambéry, who, with Jesuit acuteness, recognised immediately that this was the spirituality that the world needed and also that it was presented in a style by which the world could be converted. Therefore the Jesuits urged Francis to print these excellent and useful letters and Francis acted on their advice. He gathered his letters together, sifted them, and published them as a book entitled : *Introduction à la Vie Dévote*. This is the famous *Philothea*.

In the elegance and intimacy of his letters, Francis is speaking to the soul, and in this lies the special quality of this book which places it above other books of spiritual counsel and exhortation. One soul confronts another soul, personally and intimately. There is no incoherent mass of detached advice, no " one should do so-and-so "— vague exhortations unrelated to circumstances. In these pages Francis sees a living person before him as vividly as though he were speaking to someone. He begins his letters : My dear Philothea.

The French-speaking Catholic world acclaimed him and bought his book with the greatest eagerness. The King of France declared that it had exceeded his wildest expectations and the Queen sent a copy in a diamond-decorated binding to England. Bishops and Generals of religious orders sent congratulations and good wishes, and within a year the first edition was exhausted, and within two years the second.

The book also gave rise to criticism from the side of the " pious ". Francis himself refers to the crude censure of certain people who took offence at the modern and secular language and were angry that the judgment on dancing and merry-making was so mild. The prudery of following years omitted several passages when preparing new editions, including the whole chapter on married life. Francis endured these attacks with equanimity and often with laughter. He had written the book for a woman and Philothea was a girl's name, but Francis considered that men should not be so absurd as to object, and resolved to call the correspondent in his next book Timothy in the hope that women would be more sensible. Whatever might happen, he stood by his convictions ; what was written was written ; he did not change his book in any way and his firmness was justified by the future results. When he died the book had gone into more than fifty editions in French. In 1653 there appeared in Paris a *Philothea* in verse . . . decorated with beautiful pictures. This adaptation was symptomatic of the spirit of the age and we must excuse its error of taste. The *Introduction* has been read all over the world to-day and there are millions of copies of it. It is read in China and Mexico in the language of the people. Pius XI, in his Jubilee Encyclical of 1923, said : " May this book be read by all again to-day, as it was once. . . . Then Christian piety will flower everywhere afresh and the Church of God will be made joyful through the holiness of Her children ".[1]

[1] Encyclical *Rerum omnium perturbationem*.

Philothea belongs to the great classics of religious literature. To-day it is more than three hundred years old and it must be admitted that, like many classics, its full beauty can be assimilated only by those who take the trouble to read it with understanding and love. Much that the world of that time found thoroughly new and modern seems to us to-day to be obvious and platitudinous. The new way of life that Francis initiated at that time has become ordinary, since we have been accustomed to it from our youth. But a comparison with other religious systems of the time, and especially with that of the age immediately preceding Francis, shows clearly how bold and daring and strong his work was. Some aspects of it seem queer to the modern reader—the picture of the chaste elephant, for instance, has raised some hearty laughs ; but it was precisely this symbolism from the lives of plants and animals which enchanted the seventeenth century. It was not the outcome of direct observation of nature, nor does it show any of Francis's knowledge of nature ; but it came in part from the natural histories which were so much loved in the Middle Ages and from which the sculptors of Gothic cathedrals took their symbolism of beasts and plants ; in part from Pliny's famous *Natural History*. Francis's use of these symbols should be regarded, then, as quotations from a classical writer of Ancient Rome are regarded ; and the humanistic and educated world of his time welcomed them as such. Francis had observed people's partiality for this form of knowledge while in Paris in 1602, and he simply chose his symbolism in accordance with the literary tastes of the time in order to attain his religious objective. " I always keep the spiritual formation of our century before my mind," he said, " and it is necessary that I should do so for it is important to be perpetually aware of the century in which one is writing." Finally, when we are reading translations we must remember that the beauties of the original text are nearly always lost. The refinement of his language and the brilliant playing on words are completely lacking in translations, and the fact that no history of French literature omits his name is sufficient testimony of his artistic greatness.

Eight years later Francis published his second master-piece, the *Traitté de l'Amour de Dieu* which is also called *Timotheus*. He describes this book himself as being the history of " the birth and growth—the intensity and peculiarity—the excellence and the sublimity—of the love of God ". Since the time of Christ there has been much discussion about the Love which is the first and greatest commandment and which is at the heart of all Catholic moral theology and of all religious effort. But this centre point has been sometimes rendered invisible by the over-emphasising of the structure which underlies and surrounds it. It is Francis's great glory that he swept away these superstructures and gave men a clear view of the central point, and this he has done with more strength than any other writer, St. Augustine not excepted. Love is the alpha and omega of his life, the starting-point and the goal, and, according to him (and here he differs from many others), it is also the way to the goal. This love is the theme of his discussions with St. Jane-Frances de Chantal, and it was for this love that he wrote his book. He refers to it as " our book " in his notes to her on the progress of the work.[1]

In its wealth and depth of thought this book stands higher than the *Introduction*—too high, in fact, for the

[1] *Œuvres* Vol. XV, p. 330 ; Vol. XVI, pp. 20, 128, 140.

mass of people who for all that, and in spite of its length, read it with enthusiasm, but were not in a position to understand completely the philosophy of the Love of God or to integrate it into the daily conduct of their lives. Hence the *Traitté* became the guide-book of those with a mystical tendency while the *Introduction* became a popular book which everybody could understand and which at the same time remained entirely satisfying to the informed.

Besides these two masterpieces, which Francis himself published, we possess a collection of about 2,100 letters. These letters also are some of the finest pieces of religious literature. In the intimate style of these letters where there is no thought of the public, where there is no risk of the misunderstanding and criticism which cramps free expression, his personality unfolds in the clearest and loveliest way. In the letters to the Countess especially we see straight into the holiness of Francis's soul and find the authentic explanation of both his masterpieces. Here, in these gentle dialogues between soul and soul, we recognise the unparalleled master of spiritual direction. What was said of *Philothea* must be repeated here with even more emphasis, however : the older editions contain only an insufficient number of chosen fragments, and the translations are usually so bad that they appear as a candle to the sun of the original. Prudery and her poor relation, lack of imagination, have been the cause of numerous omissions, and an insufficient sense of language has rendered the translations almost unrecognisable. A really just appreciation or criticism depends on the reading of the original Annecy edition which alone has the true text.

There is also a vast collection of " literary remains " which fill twenty-five volumes. What a wealth of thought and labour is contained between the covers of these books ! And at the same time Francis was the bishop of a diocese whose inhabitants were torn with religious struggles and whose area stretched to Geneva in the north and to Mont Blanc in the east. He describes his bishopric as a " noble ship, battered and leaking " and he complains that " the affairs of this diocese are like a rushing stream ".[1] He founded the order of Salesian Women in 1610, always filling the office of confessor and spiritual father in the Mother-house at Anneçy himself; and he was the principal protector and supporter of the numerous new foundations throughout France. Again and again we find him journeying for months at a time through his bishopric, through France and Italy. In one day he would fulfil his duties as bishop, as kindly adviser and director of souls at the convent, and as the writer of a book on the Love of God. He was a man of strength, refinement, education, and genius. We should notice the tremendous energy with which he treats the most tender aspects of life in his writings, for it is precisely in this combination of strength and gentleness that the greatness of his personality lies. We can understand why the King of France wanted to make him court Bishop and why the Pope wanted to make him a cardinal of the Sacred Curia. But his answer to such flattering offers was always : " No ! . . . except it be for the greater honour of God I shall do nothing ". God had entrusted him with this difficult diocese which he compared with a " poor wife ", and it was His will that he should cleave to it. God's will and God's pleasure were the unique motive and the final goal of Francis's life and work.

It is not my intention to give an exhaustive account of

[1] *Œuvres*, Vol. XIII, pp. 10, 139.

his life and work. This short survey should serve as sufficient introduction to the study of his teaching. Death found him in the midst of his work. An attack of apoplexy put an end to his rich life on earth. It happened while he was travelling to Lyons on December 28th, 1622. The people of Anneçy received their dead bishop in tears and the soul that knew him best—St. Jane-Frances de Chantal—prayed to him straightway : " Thou, my father, my leader, and my saint ".

PART ONE

THE THEOLOGY OF THE SALESIAN IDEAL

(i) GOD'S PLAN

RELIGION means the binding of man with God. Every religion receives its particular stamp from its particular conception of God, mankind, and the relationship between them. This is true of paganism as well as Christianity. Similarly, if we wish to inquire, within the confines of the Catholic Church, into the religious and ethical viewpoint of any of Her saints we must begin with these primary conceptions—the nature of God, the nature of man, and the relationship between them. Now since God has created man as He has and in no other way, and since God has determined the relationship between Himself and His creatures, our first question concerns God's plan of the world.

Primitive thought always concentrates on the multiplicity of impressions. Then, by means of deep reflexion, the understanding forces its way beyond the multiplicity and onward to the organic interdependence of individuals. The final objective of all knowledge is to discover the centre-point of the whole. St. Francis de Sales, like most great thinkers, deeply desired a complete and all-inclusive view of the world. With one glance his eye swept over the totality of the universe and perceived the immeasurable wealth of natural creation—the stars and the world, land and waters, plants and animals, men and angels. And then his soul turned in faith to the endless abundance of supernatural creation—the Kingdom of Grace and Glory, the Mysteries of God's Incarnation and the Salvation of mankind, and the wonderful consequences of these two mysteries. God's image and likeness is reflected in a unique way in each individual soul of the numberless hosts of holy souls, and in spite of the differences which separate one from the other as heaven from earth, every individual element in creation is bound up with the rest in a beautiful harmony—the infinite Many is ordered for the unity of the Universe. The Universe is a " unidiverse "—a unity developed to the richest diversity, a well-ordered totality made up of endless numbers of individual parts.

This totality and unification makes one turn to the Creator. He is " Being", the completeness of Being in complete unity. In Him there is no temporal before and after, no spatial juxtaposition, no difference between Being, Thought and Will. In this unity and simplicity of His being we find the basis of the unity of the universe and of the harmonious joining of nature and supernature.

Of course God's highest unity is incomprehensible to human understanding. We can only grope our way to Him by the numberless steps of His work, and only according to the form of our knowledge of temporal and spatial relationships can we apprehend His attributes and try to reflect His unique thoughts and mysteries. We know that the idea of a before and after in time does not represent the unified nature of God. We know quite well that we are substituting the mode of thought of the human intellect, and should add at the end that in God there is no difference between essence and attribute, no distinction between yesterday and to-day, before and after. As long as we are conscious of these facts, we can speak unreflectively of God's particular thoughts and mysteries as they appear to our limited intelligences : just as we say that to-day the sun is red or yellow, dim or brilliant, knowing all the time that these changes are not in the sun but derive from the atmosphere surrounding the earth.

Having stated these principles, let us approach our question.

Why did God create the world, why the Kingdom of the Supernatural ; why did the Son of God become man, and why the Redemption of the human race ? These questions, asked in every age, were answered for Catholics by the Fathers of the Church and the Theologians. But the inquiring mind could not be content with each question separately. Ultimately, there must be a supreme idea from which the whole of God's plan can be deduced, a fundamental conception in which we may find one answer to all the individual questions.

The problem has been the source of questioning for centuries, and the further this scientific questioning proceeded, the clearer became the central question for Christian thinkers : what is the exact part played by the Incarnation of God's eternal Son in God's plan for the world ? Is it part of the plan of creation, and would it have happened if there had been no Fall and no original sin ? Or is it the result of original sin, a making-good of the disorder into which the divine order of the world was thrown by mankind ? A number of writers and Fathers of the Church think the first, and a number the second. Scholasticism systematised these diffused theories and two great schools of thought arose. The Thomist considers the Redemption as the sole object of the Incar-

nation, and the Scotist declares that the Incarnation
belongs essentially to God's plan, while the Redemption
was added to it as a result of original sin.

Obviously the uniting of the Godhead with His creature
in the unity of the Second Person is unquestionably the
greatest element in the whole work of creation. The
person of Christ is necessarily the object of the greatest
possible divine satisfaction, and each of His acts the
highest possible glorification of the Heavenly Father.
Can we therefore admit that the most stupendous act of
the love of Almighty God was only conditioned by the
fact of the Fall ? Can we concede that the highest is
conditioned by the lowest, the Incarnation of the Son of
God by the sin of His creature ? Must we really maintain that without Adam's sin, the loveliest thing in the
universe—the most intimate union of God with His
creation—would never have occurred ? Rather, are we
not forced to recognise the Incarnation of the Logos as
the corner-stone of the whole of creation ? Is it not more
suitable and probable that God intended from the very
beginning that the Incarnation of His Son should be the
completion of His work of creation ? According to this
latter theory the Fall made only one difference—that
the Son of God came into the world not as a
" homo gloriosus ", a man of glory, but as a sufferer, a Man
of Sorrows.

Honorius of Autun (died 1152) declared that sin, the
greatest evil, cannot have led to the Incarnation, but
only to the saving death of Christ. Scotus developed this
opinion into a theological system. It won numerous and
enthusiastic supporters even outside the Scotist school,
such as St. Bernardino of Siena and Suarez. St. Francis
de Sales had thought over the problem for a long time

and had carefully studied the theological arguments on both sides. Finally, he took the Scotist side, and he could hardly have done otherwise. His whole life and character were so bent on man's union with God that nothing but this belief could entirely satisfy him.

" God is Love," writes St. John, and St. Paul declares, " Christ is the first-born of every creature, for in Him were all things created in heaven, and on earth, visible and invisible . . . all things were created by Him and in Him. And He is before *all*, and by Him all things consist " (John iv, 8 and 16 ; Colossians i, 15–17). Both these conceptions form the foundation of St. Francis's outlook. God is " the unending goodness ". From its very nature, however, good must share itself. St. Thomas Aquinas indicated the goodness of God as the basis of His action. Francis now perceives the unfolding and progress of the divine will to share, and divides it into four degrees. We see God first of all in the divine nature, in the Mystery of the Trinity. " The Father communicates His whole infinite and indivisible Godhead to the Son through begetting Him ; Father and Son communicate their one Godhead to the Holy Ghost." So God's will to communicate forms the basis of the Trinity of the Persons in the unity of the divine nature. The divine goodness will, however, " enter into union outside its own nature with a creature ". Thus comes the Incarnation. A creature shall come into existence receiving the whole completeness of the Godhead. The creature is united with the Only Begotten Son of the eternal Father. Divine nature and human nature join in the unity of the person with the object that human nature " should enjoy the infinite glory of God for ever ". With this comes the God-man Jesus Christ, " *le premier en l'intention divine* ", the "*primum in intentione*", as philosophy puts it, the starting-point of the divine will to create, the goal of God's plan for the world. Hence we, with St. Paul, call Christ the "first-born of all creatures". Yet God's goodness now reaches a third degree. God's goodness is not confined to the single person of the God-man. It pours itself forth upon other creatures. God chooses "men and angels for the company of His Son". "They shall partake in His grace and glory, worship and praise Him for ever." Then for men God creates—the fourth degree—beasts and plants and the whole visible world as "*moyens naturels*", as Francis says; "the natural foundations which make it possible for mankind to glorify the goodness of God".

The God-man stands in the centre of the divine plan. God created man for the sake of Christ, and the rest of the world for the sake of man. The establishment of this conception of the cosmos led Francis on to the following psychological considerations.

The most valuable thing in the universe is the person of Christ. Every well-ordered will, and the divine will too, directs itself first of all to the Highest and then, after that, to the less important. Thus we must accept that God, in the project of His eternal plan, saw first Him Who was the most valuable and the most deserving of love—the person of the God-man; and then afterwards willed the remaining creatures, according to their nearer or further relationship to Christ. One plants a vineyard for the purpose of acquiring fruit. The fruit is the first thing wanted even though the vine produces leaves and sap before the grape finally appears. In this way Christ is the beginning and end of the divine plan. On His account "was the vineyard of the universe

planted and the succession of mankind established, which,
like leaves and sap," precede him and at the same time
prepare for the fruit, Jesus Christ, the central point of the
universe.

One Christmastide—we do not know the year—Francis
de Sales, having pondered on this, wrote it down in the
manuscript of the *Traitté*.[1] In his last Christmas sermon
(1622) he proclaimed his conviction once again : " The
Heavenly Father planned the creation of this world for
the incarnation of His Son. The end of His work was
also the beginning. Divine wisdom saw from all eternity
that the eternal Word should assume our nature and
come into this world. Before Lucifer and the world
were created, before our first parents had sinned, all this
had been determined ".[2] Three days later death led
Francis to his eternal Father.

Naturally we are free to accept or reject his teaching.
We can if we wish follow the Thomistic conception
according to which the redemption of mankind after the
Fall is the primary object of the Incarnation. But whatever we do we must recognise the beauty and completeness of the Scotist outlook from which St. Francis received
his inspiration. This outlook stands for the highest
soaring of human thought : God's goodness is the primal
source of all reality in the world, and Christ is " the
Alpha and Omega, the first and the last, the beginning
and end " of creation. The Word of the Mysterious
Revelation of St. John is revealed here in its deepest
sense.

This interpretation of the divine plan is the corner-
stone of the saint's view of ethics. It gives us the key to

---

[1] *Œuvres*, Vol. IV, p. 92.
[2] *Œuvres*, Vol. X, p. 413.

the understanding of his life and doctrine. " All is thine ; thou, however, art Christ's, and Christ is God's," writes St. Paul. Christ is the centre of the universe, for Christ's sake man was made, and for men the earth with all its excellence, teaches St. Francis de Sales. Between God and the world there is the soul. It belongs to God and all other things belong to it. Thus it embraces heaven and earth. Forgetful of the world, the soul reaches up to God, its only goal and object—the meaning of its existence. But in the fulness of this union with God, man also embraces joyfully the earth with all its beauty. It is the work of God created solely for man, as the garden in which he can mature for heaven. Love of God, and joy in God's creation go hand in hand.

It is this outlook which gives St. Francis's moral teaching its particular character. More than any other religious writer, he insists on an unresting concentration of the whole personality on the love of God. More frank than any other spiritual director, he allows the indulging in earthly pastimes and the enjoyment of the noble pleasures of the world. Ancient philosophers and gnostics had looked on God and the world as irreconcilable contradictions. With Francis this dualism is non-existent, and he will have none of any Christian thought that is tinged by it.

God Himself has bound Himself to creation in the person of Christ. For the sake of Christ man was created, and hence is established the relation of man to God and the totality of the universe. This interpretation of God's divine plan is the basis of a most beautiful conception of life in which mankind loves God above all things and takes an unrestrained joy in the things that God has made for His children.

(ii) UNION WITH GOD

The statement of St. John, " God is Love ", on which Francis's religious system is founded, stands before us clearly and vividly. This Love has selected human nature to bind itself with—in the person of the heavenly Son. Each individual man becomes the mirror of Christ. Even here below, man is to be a " partaker of the divine nature ", and afterwards partakes of God's eternal glory in heaven. " To such a noble end " are we all created— to companionship with God ; and God will find therein His honour, and we our happiness. The way to attain this end is already indicated to the soul by God's activity. God created us out of love, and through love we should unite ourselves to Him. " God, Who created men in His image and likeness, wills that, as in Him, so in men, all should be accomplished through love and for love." " The love of man for God has its cause, progress and fulfilment in the eternal love of God for man." Love is the fundamental law of the universe.[1]

In the first book of the *Traitté de l'Amour de Dieu*, Francis expounds the basis of our love of God—namely, the natural tendency of mankind towards union with God. He set about his inquiry as a psychologist, inquiring next into the nature of love itself and for this purpose observing life. Then he made use of these conclusions in the domain of the love of God.

Love seeks to become one with the beloved. It presupposes two things : the recognition of the possibility, and the yearning for the fulfilment, of this union. The achievement of this union is dependent on a certain similarity between subject and object which we call " likeness "—for, between entirely different beings, no

[1] *Œuvres*, Vol. IV, pp. 40, 231.

union can take place. Thus the possibility of union must first of all be recognised, but this recognition is not enough to awaken a longing for the union to become real. The sight of a " like " object does not necessarily incite striving and effort, for one does not long for what one possesses but rather for what one lacks, the possession of which, however, appears as a gain. The beginning of love, therefore, is not in the contemplation of similar qualities, but in the contemplation of such dissimilar qualities as are complementary to our own and the union with which will complete our own ego. Thus, likeness, " *la ressemblance* ", is not the real cause of love ; the real cause is the perception of those qualities which are harmonious, the " *correspondance et proportion* " which is basic in the idea that lovers, " through their union with one another, are each enabled to achieve completion and improvement ". " *La correspondance n'est autre chose que le mutuel rapport, qui rend les choses propres à s'unir pour s'entre—communiquer quelque perfection.*" [1]

In this conception of the fundamentals of love, Francis consciously deviates from the doctrine of Aristotle and consequently from that of St. Thomas Aquinas. Both these consider likeness to be the cause of love. " Similarity is the characteristic of all friendship," declares Aristotle. " Likeness is, properly speaking, the cause of love," says St. Thomas. Francis, characteristically, looked at practical life and considered love in its actual development, searching for the moment in which the satisfaction and longing is realised. And he sees its origin not in similar but in complementary qualities. Of course, besides actual likeness, St. Thomas also mentions potential likeness by which one lover actually possesses that which the other

[1] *Œuvres*, Vol. IV, pp. 48-50.

has only in potentiality, *i.e.*, that which he is striving after. Here the plus of one confronts the minus of the other and consequently the resultant love expresses itself as a one-sided longing. St. Francis, on the other hand, saw the essence of complementary attraction as the capacity of both lovers to be perfected through interaction in the event of a union. Francis thus deviates from the Aristotelian and Thomist theory and comes nearer to Platonism and the humanist view. This was frequently the case with him and with many of his contemporaries.

In the *Symposium*, Plato shows that the ability of shutting oneself up in a harmonious whole is the beginning of love. He explains the love between men and women, through the ancient myth of a bi-sexual being. He makes Aristophanes present the idea that in the beginning there was, besides the male and female sexes, a third sex which was composed of man and woman. Zeus had cut them apart and hence comes love because " each searches for its counter-part ". He thinks that the will strives not for what it already possesses but for the good which it lacks and which it longs to have to complete it.

Ludovicus Vivès, prince of Sixteenth-Century Spanish humanists, is of a similar opinion. Love, he declares, is not always caused by resemblance. Frequently it is the result of a certain " proportion ", a " *competentia animarum inter se* ", on the basis of which these souls desire to be united in harmony, just as numberless different notes in good music produce melody. The lover desires to be united with the beloved because he hopes that " through this contact he may himself become good ".[1] And such is the opinion of St. Francis de Sales. He uses the very same simile of music. " The harmony is made from

[1] *De Anima et Vita*, 3, pp. 2, 4.

the dissonance with which different voices answer one another so that together they mingle into melody." [1] In other respects, too, we can see a similarity between St. Francis's theory of love and the views of the great Spanish humanists. It is very probable that Francis knew Vivès' *De Anima et Vita*.

On the basis of these psychological facts Francis approaches the relationship of man to God. God's eternal plan had destined man to the deepest companionship with Himself. It was to this end that God laid the psychological bases for such a companionship in human nature—by creating man in His likeness and thus making this companionship possible. Man's whole nature is such that he can only find full satisfaction in God and hence comes the longing to unite himself to God.

" Let us make man in our own image and likeness," says God, in the account of the creation. But because God is pure spirit it follows that man's special likeness to God lies in his soul. " The soul is spirit indivisible and immortal ; it possesses understanding and will and moreover its will is free. In that it has likeness to God. It lives wholly in the whole of its body and wholly in every part, just as the Godhead is wholly in the whole world and wholly in each part of the world." Francis, like the Fathers of the Church and the theologians of the Middle Ages, refers to the parallel between the soul and the Trinity. " Analogously the Son proceeds from the Father as His expressed knowledge, and the Holy Ghost from the Father and Son as their mutual love," and nevertheless these three different Persons are " inseparably one ".

In writings of the Fathers we come across an attempt to

[1] *Œuvres*, Vol. IV, p. 49.

extend man's likeness to God to the body as well as the soul. Philo's doctrine formed a basis for this. This Jewish philosopher strained the expression in *Genesis* about God making man in His own image, and thought that we must differentiate between image and imitation. The image of God came first of all and then man was created as an imitation of this prototype. This outlook was adopted by Clement of Alexandria and Origen. They saw the true image of God as the divine Logos and man as a copy of this bearing the form of the Logos. It is true that both ecclesiastical writers limited the likeness to the soul, but other authors extended it to the body. St. Irenæus, for instance, said " Man is like to God not only as to his soul but also as to his corporeal form ". Tertullian has the same opinion. The earth, according to Tertullian, from which God formed Adam " took on in flesh the image of the future Christ ". Thus, at the end of the Second Century, the view was current that the Incarnation of the Son of God was foreseen in God's eternal plan and the first man's body and soul was formed in imitation of the prototype which was Christ's manhood.

St. Francis de Sales, however, did not make use of this theory, though it would have fitted well into his doctrine of God's plan. For him the great question was to show that the love of God was according to nature. Therefore he showed that the soul has a likeness to God and hence is capable of union with Him. He added that there is such an attraction to God in the natural predisposition of the soul that by virtue of his very essence man must long for God because God is truly " the God of the human heart ".[1]

---

[1] *Œuvres*, Vol. IV, p. 74.

Dionysius the Areopagite, whose works form the basis of scholastic and mystical theology concerning man's union with God, explained the creature's striving for God in terms of the longing for beauty and goodness. These ideas of the " *divin saint Denis* " were taken over by St. Francis although their authenticity had already been severely questioned by the humanists. " Everything happens because of the good and the beautiful ", he says, " the beautiful draws all things towards it and all things turn towards the good." " Everything is stimulated by the good and the beautiful." As " the sun, the source of physical light ", lights up the whole universe through its beauty, and through its goodness draws to itself all the effort and all the craving of the physical world, so " God, the Father of all light " attracts the spiritual world through His beauty and goodness. God as epitome of the beautiful fills the intellect with rapture, and as epitome of the good fills the will with love. Hence all spiritual life susceptible of beauty and goodness strives towards God.[1]

Every soul has a tendency towards God. " Every man knows it . . . and nobody can deny it." Owing to the manifold nature of earthly impressions, this predisposition of the soul often remains unperceived. It can happen, and repeatedly does happen, that this " *correspondance* " is not realised in the din of life. " Like a chicken under the wings of a hen " so " our heart is hatched under the wings of nature, nourished and elevated in the midst of physical, worthless, and ephemeral things." But with the first sight of God and the first knowledge obtained of Him, its original natural predisposition to love God is awakened. Observation of life and experience show that

Œuvres, Vol. V, pp. 22 *sq.*

" as soon as man recalls the Godhead a certain sweet movement fills his heart. . . . Our understanding has never such great joy as when thinking of God ". Human intelligence confesses with Aristotle, " the prince of philosophers ", that " the smallest knowledge of the Godhead is more valuable than the greatest knowledge of all other things ". And " if our heart gets alarmed over some event or other then it flies immediately to the Godhead and therewith recognises that God alone is good, if all else opposes it ". This joy in the knowledge of God and trust in His goodness derive from the soul's natural inclination to God.[1]

As proof of man's theocentric inclination, Francis refers to the pre-Christian philosophers. An enthusiastic humanist himself, he skilfully brings the humanistic enthusiasm of his contemporaries into the service of religion. The pagan philosophers, he maintains, exhibited " not only a great knowledge of God, but also a strong inclination towards Him ". " Socrates, most esteemed amongst them, had a clear knowledge of God's unity and his inclination to love God was so great that, as many authors declare, he only had one object in teaching moral philosophy which was to purify the soul so that it could the better contemplate the highest good ". Plato declared that " a philosopher is nothing else than a lover of God ". A similar struggle of the human soul to gain the companionship of God can be seen in the Stoics, in Seneca, and above all in Epictetus, whom Francis especially treasured and admired. Of course it must be said that the human spirit, weakened by sin, is unable to reach the longed-for goal. " Like palm-trees, they only sprout incompletely, trying, so to speak, to produce fruit

---

[1] *Œuvres*, Vol. IV, pp. 74, 79.

without maturing the ripe dates." Similarly man never gets beyond a certain beginning of the love of God with his own strength. But " from nature itself we feel the predisposition to love God above all things ", and we experience " the thirst after costly water ". And " this inclination shows that we belong to our creator " and that " our heart is created for God ".[1]

A clear proof of the soul's desire to be incorporated with God is seen in our longing for the infinite. The desire of our understanding to know is unlimited and tends to penetrate deeper and deeper into the kingdom of truth. The will's hunger for the good is insatiable. " Nothing on earth could satisfy the soul ", the whole universe is incapable of satisfying its power of comprehension, for " our heart is greater than the world ", hence our soul thirsts ceaselessly for eternity. The human soul calls from the depths of its being : " I am not created for this world. There is a highest good from which I depend, an infinite Master Who has implanted in me this boundless yearning for knowledge and this unconquerable longing. I must struggle towards Him, stretch upwards so as to unite myself in all ardour with His goodness to which I belong in an especial way ".[2]

Joyful giving and receiving are characteristics of the relationship between God and man. " The One ", says Francis, " has a great superabundance and a great desire to give the good, and the other has a great need and great desire to receive it." God's joy and glory lie in this distribution of His gifts, but in it man finds his yearning stilled and his essence completed. This is the relationship, says Francis, in which we stand to God.

[1] Œuvres, Vol. IV, pp. 80–83, 85 ; Vol. XIII, p. 133.
[2] Œuvres, Vol. IV, pp. 76 sq. ; Vol. XII, p. 203 ; Vol. XIV, p. 395.

The saint returns repeatedly in his meditations to this teleological attitude. Time and time again his glance is turned to this corner-stone of Christian life : created by God—destined for God. A fine, poetical perception lights up his presentation of the theory. " Towards this rivers flow ceaselessly, and bend, as the philosopher says, back to the place of their origin. The sea, the place of their birth, is also the place of their last rest. All their movement has only one object which is to unite itself with their source." " O God, thou hast created my heart for Thee ", says St. Augustine, " and therefore it can never find peace except in Thee ". Francis adopts these ideas and praises a holy restlessness for God. " O wonderful restlessness of the human heart. Be always without rest, O my soul, and without resting-place on this earth until thou hast rediscovered the fresh waters of immortal life in the most holy Godhead Who alone can bring thy restlessness to peace and thy yearning to realisation." He looks forward with joy to the day of realisation. " O, how our hearts will be united with God there in heaven where, after these unending yearnings which are never stilled here below, we shall find the living and mighty source of the true good." [1]

As a consequence of these primary Catholic truths we can say that man is created by God and for God. On the last day of creation it will be discovered what man should be according to God's eternal plan ; but that which man is now, is already forcing him onwards to God from the very definition of his nature. The *should be* is a result of the *be*. One should be holy—that is, bound up with God —just as one should be healthy. The moral *ought* corresponds to the physical *ought* of our being, for our nature

[1] *Œuvres*, Vol. IV p. 199.

has been so made by the Creator that it strives upwards to Him and finds its completion in Him. Considered in the first way, the natural law of conscience is nothing else than God's eternal will ; but considered in the second, this law, because it " was written in our hearts ", appears as the moral law of the human soul. Autonomy and heteronomy are fused into one. There is no question, of course, as St. Francis himself declares, that as a result of original sin " the perfect realisation of the commandments does not lie in the scope of human strength ; nevertheless this perfect realisation remains within the borders of human instinct as something responding to the natural light of reason. We are not going outside our natural inclination if we live according to God's commandments ".

Our task in life could be described briefly as the movement from existence to quality, from the embryonic to the fully conscious realisation of Christ's image in our own selves. The development of an individual who is fully conscious of his end, according to the will of God, leads necessarily to realising the complete man as well as the complete saint. *Nihil humani a me alienum puto* was the way Terence put it—nothing human is outside my interests. This sentiment was a blow to the rigorists who had become estranged from the world, but it was a joy to the humanists. For St. Francis de Sales it was a perfect expression of his conviction that the completed Christian is also the most noble of men. " *Je suis tant homme que rien plus* ", he says of himself [1] (I am a man through and through), and in his writing he preached unceasingly the fusion of devotion and humanity as the ethical ideal.

But if, as we have said, the consequence of the unceasing

[1] *Œuvres*, Vol. XIII, p. 330.

fulfilment of God's will is the highest development of man who has been created according to God's will, then religious achievement must also guarantee the highest gratification of mankind and assure a happy life. Aristotle started his inquiry into ethics with man's desire for happiness, and St. Thomas followed the same line of thought in the *Summa*. Francis was in convinced agreement with this doctrine of traditional philosophy and theology. " There are three goods that we should strive after : the honourable, the useful, and the pleasant." We find them in virtue : " only virtue and devotion can satisfy the soul in the world . . . the further one's progress in virtue, the greater one's happiness ". " O devout life, how beautiful you are, how pleasant and how lovable." [1]

Hence because of his inner tendency to companionship with God, the completed saint is the completed man. He is also the happiest of men and the greatest glorification of God because in his personality he realises what God intended in creation. This doctrine meant, for St. Francis de Sales and his contemporaries, that the gulf was bridged between Christianity and humanism. Besides the historical importance of these statements, their permanent value lies in the fact that they form the basis of the great synthesis of the two fundamental strivings, self-development and surrender to God ; and this synthesis alone answers to the unified essence of human nature.

(iii) ORIGINAL SIN

Against the ideal of the dependence of human nature on God, as described above, the objection could be raised that this relationship was severely shaken as a result of the Fall, and such an objection is perfectly justifiable. The idea of original sin and the extent of the ruin which it brought on mankind is bound to influence profoundly the conception of God and man and the relationship between them.

History shows us two extreme trends of thought which both ended in heresy. The underestimation and even the complete disavowal of original sin and its results can be seen, in ancient days, with the Pelagians, and in modern times with Rousseau and the philosophers following the French Revolution. They misunderstood the moral weakness of human nature and forgot the evil force which militates against the predisposition towards goodness given us by God. The theory of education which went with this was based on the axiom " follow your inclinations ". The consequence of this teaching is bound to be moral depravity because the tares grow up as luxuriantly as the wheat. The heresies of the Reformation and Jansenism, on the other hand, erred in the opposite direction. According to them the fall meant complete corruption and there was no more belief in man's goodness. The result was either an abandonment of any personal striving after moral perfection, or the killing of all enjoyment in life and God and the substitution of a deadly rigorism. Luther took the first way and Jansenius took the second, while the Catholic Church held fast to the truth that none of human nature's natural predispositions had been annihilated by original sin. With regard to the question of how far these predispositions were weakened and wounded opinions differed in Catholic circles as elsewhere. In order to understand the wide division of opinion one need only compare the pessimistic doctrine of St. Augustine with the optimism of St. Robert Bellarmine. The very comparisons which were used to illustrate the actual condition of fallen man and his theoretical natural condition show clearly the clash of the two schools of thought. The supporters of rigorism maintained that the relationship was the same as that between " a healthy man and a sick man ", while their opponents declared that the difference was no greater than that between " a clothed and an unclothed man ". In the early Middle Ages there was a tendency towards the pessimism of St. Augustine. The optimistic opinion got its first support in the golden age of scholasticism, the theological treatises of which were based on Aristotelian philosophy. It celebrated its victory with the theologians of the Sixteenth Century who were of humanist upbringing. The extreme and heretical reaction against this increased optimism was attempted by Baïus but was condemned by the Church.

St. Francis de Sales accepted the optimistic point of view. His acceptance was prompted by his humanist education, for he knew the yearning for God of the heathen philosophers, and his reverence for Bellarmine strengthened his conviction. He carried Bellarmine's controversies about with him as a young missionary and later he became a friend of the author's. But he was really driven to his opinion by the realisation that the God of love had, in spite of His omniscience and foreknowledge of the Fall, nevertheless created man. Francis believed in and trusted human goodness. This is brought out in countless remarks throughout his works and in his method of spiritual direction. We must keep these facts permanently before our eyes if we are going to understand the saint's ideas about the Fall. Besides these mainly optimistic expressions, however, we find a few other remarks amongst which the axiom of the schools *Natura est . . . vulnerata in naturalibus*—nature is wounded in what is natural—as well as the sentence added on to the story of the Good Samaritan by the early scholastics, *homo est semivivus relictus*—the man was left half-dead—which remind one of the rigoristic theology. In the *Traitté* Francis rejects the doctrine of the Reformers who said that " the sinner is in a similar condition to the devil whose will is so seized by, and permeated with, evil that he can do no good whatever ". But he refers then to the gospel story of the man who went from Jerusalem to Jericho, fell among thieves, and was left half-dead. " In the same way," says Francis, " the natural reason is deeply wounded and as if half-dead as a result of sin." In a sermon of the year 1619 Francis declares that " sin has spoilt and wounded our inner strength to such a degree that the lower part of our soul usually has more strength to draw us to evil than the higher part has to strengthen us in our striving Godwards ". In both places we see unmistakably the influence of the maxims of the school mentioned above. In the first-quoted phrase he goes on immediately to say " therefore in this evil condition reason cannot carry out all the commandments of God although it knows very well that they are appropriate and answering to our needs. . . . Of course the sinner can observe a few commandments in particular cases or even all for a short time. But that he should persevere for a long time without committing new sins is impossible without special aid from God ". Therefore Christ makes the appeal to personal activity : " watch and pray ". The second phrase occurs in a sermon on monastic life, and is followed by the declaration : " hence it is very suitable that we should bind ourselves to God's will by the vow of obedience . . . which will be shown to us through His commandments and counsels, through our rules and through the counsels of our superiors ".[1] Francis de Sales seems to emphasise the corruption of human nature so much here that rigoristic opinion could be derived from these phrases as from others.

The ruinous consequences of original sin, according to Francis's doctrine, firstly attack the " lesser part of our soul "—the " sensitive forces and especially the imagination ", and the " sensual cravings which we call concupiscence " ; and in the second place the will which no longer has the strength to bring these lesser forces to quick and docile obedience. The reason is damaged, and the darkened understanding supports itself by concentrating on the lesser powers of the soul, especially the imagination. Therefore we must all complain with the Apostle of the Gentiles " that we think not on the good that we love but on the evil that we hate ". Nevertheless reason knows that God is the end and that following the commandments is the means to the end ; " it knows its duty " but the will lacks the strength to carry it out. " The eyes," declares Francis, " have more vision for seeing the right way than the legs have strength for following it." [2]

" Although our human nature no longer possesses the original health and uprightness which the first man had at his creation, and although we are badly corrupted through sin, nevertheless we still retain the instinct to love God above all things, and the natural light through which we recognise that divine goodness is lovable beyond all else."[3] To follow the leadership of this knowledge

[1] Œuvres, Vol. V, p. 238.
[2] Œuvres, Vol. IV, pp. 27 sq
[3] Œuvres, Vol. IV, p. 78

and love is no longer within the scope of man's unaided
strength. But it is here that the grace of God comes in.
It was God's divine will to share with us, that determined
the incarnation of the Son of God. The Son of God, made
man, brought redemption to fallen man. St. Francis de
Sales now proceeds to the consequences of the doctrines
we have considered, and these consequences are surpris-
ingly great. " God's healing love had more power to
save man than Adam's unhappy fall had venomous
strength to annihilate him. Adam's sin could in no way
prevail against God's goodness ; on the contrary, it
helped it onwards and inflamed it." The God-man
undertook the redemption " because all were dead " :
therefore He died for all. " Where sin prevailed there also
was grace abounding," and Francis refers to the solemn
words of the liturgy of Holy Saturday " O truly necessary
sin of Adam, which through Christ's death was blotted
out ! O happy fault, which merited so great a
redeemer ! "

Francis joins in with this *O felix culpa* in enthusiastic
conviction. " Really, Timotheus, we can say with that
man of olden days "—he is referring to Themistocles—
" we were lost if we had not been lost for our loss brought
us gain." In reality human nature has received more
grace through the Redemption of the Saviour than it
would have obtained had Adam remained guiltless, and
though Divine Providence has ordained that the deep
traces of the first sin's severity should remain—the
necessity of death, sickness and concupiscence—yet
God's heavenly graciousness predominates over everything. He turns all these hardships to the greatest use
of those who love Him. The virtue of patience springs
from drudgery, contempt of the world from the necessity of

death, and a thousand victories are won in fighting concupiscence. According to Pliny's story, if a rainbow touches a bush called the Aspalatus it exhales a fragrance lovelier than lilies. So the redemption of our Lord touches our misery and greater use and greater loveliness come from it than would have existed in a condition of guiltlessness. According to the teaching of Our Lord, there is more joy in heaven over a sinner who does penance than over ninety-nine righteous men who need no penance. So, also, the condition of being redeemed is a hundred times more valuable than the condition of guiltlessness. " Sprinkled with the blood of Our Lord . . . we recovered a purity incomparably lovelier than the pure snow of guiltlessness." Like Naaman, we stepped purer and more whole from the stream of salvation than if we had never suffered from leprosy. As God's majesty commands us, " allow yourself not to be conquered by evil but conquer evil by good, as God Himself was not overcome by evil but overcame evil through good. . . . His loving-kindness stands over the righteous. . . . His compassion reigns over all His works ".[1]

This healthy optimism, of course, is not new. It was there in antiquity. But no theologian, until Francis, had dared to praise the redemption so strongly and understandingly. It is here that Francis's fundamental conception of God as love reaches its utmost implications. Though Augustine had conceived of love as the pivot of Christian teaching, he did not dare to apply this idea to his judgment on man fully. He was prevented from doing so by the sad experiences of his youth and by the attitude of struggle which he had to adopt against the

[1] *Œuvres*, Vol. IV, pp. 103–105.

Pelagians. But Francis's religious development is marked by no break, no sudden conversion from sinfulness to holiness. It looks almost as if youthful purity and religious development along a straight line form the natural prelude to a happy conception of religion, while the son who has been lost and found again generally inclines towards pessimism. Francis was an opponent of the radical pessimism of the Reformation and thus he goes beyond Augustine's pessimistic outlook on man. He affirms with all his strength that man is good and capable of that inner development which leads to union with God. The harm done by original sin has been more than abundantly compensated by the grace of salvation.

Looked at constructively, Francis's optimism rests on two fundamental beliefs. The first of these is the distinction between a lower and a higher part of the soul. The natural damage wrought in man by original sin is primarily in the " lesser part of our soul ". He wrote to a nun, " you have two women in you " ; one is " the daughter of Eve and hence of evil character ", but the other " . . . has the will to obey God entirely . . . is the daughter of the Blessed Virgin Mary and therefore full of good endeavour. These two daughters with such different mothers struggle with one another and the worthless one is so bad that the other often has her work cut out to defend herself against her ". Francis warns the nun about over-emphasising the evil in mankind : " this evil woman is not stronger than you ".[1] Francis identifies good with the personality itself and rejects evil as something essentially foreign to the higher man. He justifies this in the second fundamental belief : the

[1] *Œuvres*, Vol. XVI, p. 242.

doctrine of the redemption and the emphasis on God's saving grace which comes to every man's aid.

Contemporary theology had inquired into the nature and reality of the saving grace of God and the Council of Trent had defined these dogmas and presented them as Catholic belief. Unfortunately the period that followed moved away from this favourable estimate of human nature. A few writers had exaggerated the optimism, and the old traditional pessimism was still there. P. de Bérulle, Francis's contemporary, adopted as motto for his religious system : " God is everything and man is nothing ". Man is " the lowest and most useless of all creatures ".[1] The tendency to humiliate and abase mankind is very obvious here, and it is easy to see how false this exaggeration is, for nobody would seriously place man amongst the animals. Nevertheless the description " the least of all creatures " found disciples once again, and a reaction against optimism began, ending in an extreme, in heresy. History shows that that appears to be the fate of every reaction. Like a pendulum, things swing from one extreme to the other. Jansenism entirely forgot the good and only recognised the evil in human nature. In contradiction to Francis, the personality was identified with the " lower man ". The effect was necessarily a dismal austerity and a rigid harshness. Who can estimate the number of religious efforts destroyed by that Jansenist winter in the Seventeenth and Eighteenth Centuries—in that gloomy hopelessness and resignation ? It was only in the second half of the Nineteenth Century that a new springtime began to flower. Lacordaire in France and Faber in England favoured the optimistic

---

[1] P. Pourrat, *La Spiritualité chrétienne* (Paris, 1927–1931), Vol. III, p. 493 ; Vol. IV, p. 14.

outlook, and the religious literature of our time clearly adheres to that point of view. So now we can expect a new summer of religious culture. The observation of life as well as the observation of history forces us to admit that pessimism easily leads to shrinking and narrowness, but optimism in the sense of St. Francis de Sales leads to the development and broadening of our religious and moral life.

PART TWO

TWO CHARACTERISTICS OF SALESIAN RELIGIOUS LIFE

(i) OPTIMISM AND JOY

(a) Optimism and Pessimism in Religion

IT is evident and quite in accordance with reality that in the pre-Christian epoch religious thought and life was governed by the consciousness of human weakness and sinfulness. An unending gulf yawned between the God, the All-holiest, and man, His impure creature. The recognition of this fact and the consequence of it—the fear of God—appear as the characteristics of Old Testament religion. With the passing of time, however, Christ, the God-man, bridged the gulf between Creator and creature. He consummated the Redemption from sin. "Be ye perfect", said He to His disciples, and taught them to pray "Our Father". A love like the love between father and child now became the bond between God and man.

There are two possible attitudes for the believing soul. First, a feeling of distance and fear and, second, love and a joyful union with God. The psalm *Miserere* could be taken as the typical expression of the first attitude, and the *Magnificat* of Our Lady as the expression of the second. But however much these attitudes may be separated subjectively it is false to set them in any harsh historical or racial contradiction with one another. It is untrue

to claim that the first is Semitic and the second Aryan.
It would also be exaggerated to assign one exclusively
to the Old Testament and the other to the New Testament. We are prevented from classifying them in this
way by the knowledge that the God of the old Testament
was depicted as being in a marriage relationship with His
chosen people. In Hosea we find a tender love as the
bond of union, and also in *the Song of Songs* and in
Psalm xliv. In the course of the Second Century both
points of view find their particular advocates in the
writings of the Fathers. Tertullian, the former Roman
attorney, used his cool juridical way of thinking to depict
the relationship between God and man. God is the
highest ruler and judge and man as his creature has to
serve him willy-nilly like a slave : " Fear is the basis of
salvation ". " Man's fear is God's honour." His contemporary, Clement of Alexandria, sets out from the
principle that God is the good. God used his almighty
power and created the world so as to show His goodness
upon us. " We, His children, receive the best and surest
place in the work of creation." God loves everything
which came into being through Him " but more than all
He loves man. . . . His most beautiful creation ".
" Just as fathers and mothers gaze on their children with
solemn joy . . . so the Heavenly Father gazes on His
devout children. He loves, supports, and cherishes them
and calls them with tenderness, child." From this arises
man's proper attitude to God. " We must know that we
belong to Him and that we are His loveliest possessions."
Therefore man must have trust in God, love God the
Lord, and consider that as life's task. Loving trust and
joy in God are the outstanding characteristics of this way
of devotion. Clement quotes the phrase of *Genesis :* " the

King saw Isaac play with his wife ". In a subtle piece of interpretation he gives the mystical sense of this text : " the King looks on and the soul of the child in Christ is filled with joy. What is more fitting for a completely wise man than to play and be joyful . . . in a festival enjoyed with God ! . . . Christ is the King Who sees our laughter from above. Looking through the window, as the Scripture says, he perceives our homage and praise, our joy and jubilation ".

Clement and Tertullian were Christians of the same epoch, and yet in religious outlook they were very different from each other. And just as in the Second and the Third Centuries, so throughout history, we see both these outlooks flowing onwards like two mighty streams. With the Fathers of the Church, in the Middle Ages and in modern times, we always meet both with the pessimistic conception with its austerity and the optimistic conception with its joyous love. Just as our cathedrals were often begun in Roman style and completed in Gothic, and sometimes clothed yet again in the Renaissance or Baroque style, so, too, we see how both these outlooks contributed to the building of the cathedral of Christian piety. Prayer, too, took on at one time a mournful and at another time a joyful character, and was sometimes even begun under one influence and finished under the other. Karl Adam once remarked that the liturgy of the Mass was drawn up under the influence of a feeling of guilt and of distance from God. In the Ninth, Tenth and Eleventh Centuries various prayers of self-accusation were incorporated into the liturgy and later the bulk of them were rejected again. Our *Confiteor* is a survival from that time. Or let us look at the *Hail Mary* from this point of view. It is obviously composed of two parts. The first half, authenticated since the Sixth Century in the East and since the Ninth in the West, greets the Mother of God in the words of the Archangel and St. Elizabeth. But the second half, which was added on in the Fourteenth Century, speaks solely of the wonder at Mary's very beautiful and holy soul ; there is no word about one's own ability to strive or develop or seek for holiness. On the contrary, the beauty of Mary produces pessimism in the person praying and he considers his own sinfulness and looks on the hour of death and judgment with fear. And so the joyous greeting is followed by the mournful supplication : " pray for us sinners ". For a long time it was strengthened in the German to : " pray for us poor sinners ". This continuation of the *Hail Mary* is met with first in the austere order of the Carthusians and with the great penitential preacher Bernardino of Siena. The time when this addition was made a part of the prayer for everyone was also the time in which there were quantities of writings about the " art of dying well ", and the dance of death was frequently painted and acted. At that same time the deathwatch beetle was put on tombstones and death was always depicted as a corpse with a slit-open stomach or as a horrible skeleton. This figure of death was always sculped on the clocks of the period.

Another interesting illustration of the changes that occur in religious outlook is provided by the position in which people prayed. In ancient days people prayed with their arms stretched up to heaven, or extended in the shape of a cross. These wide gestures were gradually narrowed down ; they gave way to the position taken by the priest during the Prayers in the Mass, and after that the arms were crossed over the breast—a position recommended by the Carthusians. The form of folding the hands was taken from German law : the vassal lays his folded hands in those of the lord as a sign of humble submission to his service and protection. This way of establishing one's vassaldom became the customary attitude of prayer in the Middle Ages. The wide out-stretched gestures disappeared completely and were replaced by the narrow, compressed attitude. To-day, however, it is psychologically undeniable that there is a connection between our inner condition and our outer gestures, and that " the inner inspiration expresses itself in the outer attitude " or, *vice versa*, that the physical attitude of the body affects the spiritual condition. It must also be admitted that the mediæval attitude to God—that of a joyous and free child ready to receive from his God—degenerated into the cowering fear of a servant before his Lord. We have no desire to overlook the fact that other influences were at work to change the attitude of prayer ; it was discovered, for example, that wide-outstretched gestures were not suitable for community service. Moreover, the open and demonstrative exhibi-tion of one's inmost feelings is in contradiction to human reserve : we do not want to make public the relationship between God and our soul. But the fact remains : the different attitudes of prayer correspond with differences of religious temperament. We must not fail to recognise the importance of the joyful prayer that is made with arms outstretched, and we must maintain it for private recol-lection alone in our room. It alone is a fitting attitude for the *Magnificat*, for example, and we can and ought to practise it, as the saints have shown us.

It would be very interesting to study the causes which led, at one time to the pre-eminence of the optimistic outlook, and at another time to that of the pessimistic.

But to do this would lead us too far away from our subject. We may perhaps mention one thing which up to now appears to have been ignored : the more man's outlook on religion was based on the surrounding world of king and bondman, and the legal manner of thinking that went with it, the more there is a tendency to fasten on to the Old Testament idea and the pessimistic outlook that it causes. The early mediæval penitential books with their dependence on secular law, and the admonishments of certain early scholastics to do penance for known and even unknown sins, point in this direction. But the more religious thought was influenced by the Gospels and especially the Gospel of St. John, the more people felt themselves as children of the " Father in Heaven " and there was a change-over to optimism. In antiquity this is proved by a number of patristical texts, notably those of Clement of Alexandria and St. Ambrose ; and in the Middle Ages it is shown by the joyous attitude of St. Francis of Assisi and his companions. The writings of the mystics, moreover, are usually filled with the same spirit.

But this outlook was applied to thought and to life most logically of all by St. Francis de Sales. The guiding idea of the love of God logically leads him to optimism. Of course Francis was not without deep experience of human weakness and the curse of evil, and he complained strongly of our sinfulness. In his meditation on the last judgment he describes the majesty of the great Judge : " Tremble at the thought of this last day and abominate thy sins ". Francis, like St. Ignatius of Loyola, gives us no word of comfort : at this juncture in the soul's way of purification it should taste all the frightfulness of sin. But the meditation on the last judgment and hell is followed immediately by the chapter *On Paradise*, our heavenly fatherland. At the end of his mournful meditations he turns a trustful glance on the Redeemer. He says expressly in a letter that " the meditations on the four last things must end in hope and trust in God, not in fear and terror. If they were to end in fear then they would be dangerous, especially the meditation on death and hell ".[1]

The normal attitude of the soul to God, according to Francis's teaching, is the attitude of a child to its father. Tertullian's austerity had led him to describe the relationship between God and man as similar to that of master and slave. Many authors went still further and likened the relationship to that of master and dog. Francis, in sharp contrast to this, declares that the relationship between soul and God is like that between king and queen. In a letter of 1604 he consoled an ill woman by saying : " As Our Lord hung on the cross, He was declared King by His enemies. The souls which suffer under a cross are declared queens ". In the *Introduction* he describes the soul by using the simile of a young princess who was loved most tenderly by her consort. In the *Traitté* this comparison is carried still further with all the art of his style. He relates a parable, " because this mode of presentation was so pleasing to the highest Master of love ".

" A great and proud king had espoused a young and exceedingly lovely princess. One day he led her to a quiet conversation in a withdrawn chamber. Scarcely had he spoken when he saw her turn pale and faint in lifelessness. Deeply frightened he nearly fell down in a swoon himself, for he loved her more than his life. But the very love which caused him such frightful pain gave him gradually the strength to bear his pain. It awakened his energy. As quickly as possible he tried to cure the

[1] *Œuvres*, Vol. XII, pp. 333 *sq.*

sickness of his life-companion. Quickly he opened a chest and took out some fabulously expensive cordial water, filled his mouth with it, forced open the compressed lips of his deeply-loved princess and trickled the costly water from his mouth into hers. He besprinkled her forehead with the rest of the flask, moistened her temples and her heart until she finally came back to consciousness. . . . Softly he lifted her up . . . slowly she herself raised herself to her feet and trod cautiously up and down, but not without his help. . . . Gradually, as she regained her former strength, she was able to walk again unaided. Her loving consort no longer held her so fast. His hand lay softly in her hand, his arm was folded loosely round her waist."

"The soul", says Francis, "which is in a condition of goodness is the bride of Our Lord. . . . If it commits a sin, then it falls into a swoon." The God-man was "so moved by this misfortune that He died on the cross so as to redeem us from sin". But now it is no longer necessary for his love to be before us in the shape of death, though "He hastens to help the soul". With unparalleled pity he opens the door of our hearts by means of reproaches of conscience . . . and wholesome thoughts. . . . As though with sweet-smelling and reviving water, he brings the soul back to itself. . . . The soul now willingly follows the stimulation of grace. "*Si l'âme*", Francis plays on words, "*adjoute son consentement au sentiment de la grâce*", then God leads it "by the incitement of belief, hope and penitence, back to true spiritual repentance and to love". Then once again the soul can "go by itself and keep on its feet owing to the health and the gift of holy love put in its heart by the Holy Ghost".[1]

[1] *Œuvres*, Vol. IV .pp. 174–176.

The soul is not a slave but the bride of God.   In spite of the Fall and original sin and of all the sins which the soul itself has committed, it is a queen and a princess. For the love of the King has redeemed it on the cross and restored it to its former health—what Francis, alluding to the doctrine of the Fall, calls " the first health " —which it had lost.   " Ourselves are heavenly ", he says, and because of this we can and ought to be joyful ; the consciousness of it should give us courage and energy.

It is understandable that during the next ten years the pessimists, whatever their gradations and colours, were scandalised by this doctrine of St. Francis de Sales.   They bewailed its lack of " respect for God ".   " Many people may love God ", they said, " but they preserve too little awe before Him."   " Our Lord is frequently considered as Father, Redeemer and Bridegroom, but seldom as our God, Ruler and Judge."   They felt that St. Francis's attitude ruined the necessary foundation of humility and the trembling of the soul before God's majesty.   St. Cyran publicly complained that " though Francis, with his views, may have become a saint, his method is destined to spoil many souls ", and, moreover, had already " directed many to ruin ".[1] The sources of this pessimism are obviously the old ones—an idea of God which over-emphasises the " ruler and judge ", and a system of devotion whose centre is self-abasement rather than love. This attitude culminated in Jansenism, which omitted all comforting truths in opposition to it.   This radicalism was condemned as heresy by the Church.

But if we compare a measured and thoroughly orthodox pessimism with the system of St. Francis de Sales, we can observe that out saint's view is more in keeping with the

[1] Pourrat, *op. cit.*, Vol. III, pp. 507 *sq.* ; Vol. IV, pp. 20, 33.

spirit of Jesus in the first commandment, in the beatitudes
of the Sermon on the Mount, and in the only prayer He
taught His disciples : " Thus should ye pray ; Our
Father." He is called " Father ", not Lord or Ruler or
Judge. The name of Father is Christ's normal description of God. The essential attitude of the Christian to
God is shown clearly enough by this fact.

(b) Humility and Confidence

From this point of view it is worth studying exactly
in what the Christian consciousness consists. Patristical and scholastic teaching contrasted human sinfulness
with God's gifts, describing the first as the foundation of
Christian humility and self-abasement and the second
as the basis of Christian confidence. St. Augustine wrote :
" you should hate your own work in yourself, and love
God's work in you." In his *Confessions* he proclaims to
the world that " all sins and faults are my own, all that
is valuable in me is the gift of God ". Hence the *Confessions* is the first autobiography in the history of the
world which is not dedicated to self-deification and self-
justification, but to the avowal of one's own sinfulness.
Scholasticism took over St. Augustine's doctrine, but
fused it with Aristotle. " Man can be considered in two
ways ", says St. Thomas, " according as what is of God
and what is of man ". Of man is every imperfection,
of God is every perfection and all the means of salvation.
The consideration of our own weakness and insufficiency
weighs us down. " *Humilis dicitur humi acclinis* "—humble
means bowed to the ground—said Isidor of Seville. The
contemplation of God's gifts, however, makes our eyes
look upwards. It fires us to an enthusiastic striving for

every sort of greatness, and brings about an implicit trust in God's aid. Also it becomes the basis on which the Aristotelian megalopsychia (self-confidence) flourishes as a Christian virtue. The truly Christian consciousness contains both humility, as a consequence of our sins, and confidence, because of God's gifts.

Christianity has often been reproached for too great an emphasis on man's guilt and weakness. In this general form the complaint is false, but a certain one-sided over-emphasis on the part of certain writers cannot be denied. The late mediæval writers for example—and this is where the reproach is most justified—were very fond of the pessimistic tone, whose source was, of course, St. Augustine. If we glance at such writers—most of whom are unknown —we will find at the centre the *Imitation of Christ*. One of these authors had drawn up the plan for this whole system of thought : " Meditation begets knowledge, knowledge begets great sorrow, and this begets devotion ". The content of meditation is self-contemplation and the result of this is self-prostration. Could we say that the devotion resulting from this corresponds to the Salesian conception of devotion—which is the overflowing of an active love of God ? No, its origin is clear. " Piety is a pious and humble affection for God, humble because of the consciousness of one's own weakness, and pious because of the awareness of God's grace." [1]

There are two ideas here, first the acknowledgment of our weakness, poverty and nothingness ; and second the recognition of God's goodness, kindness and omnipotence. The lifting up of the heart to God is supposed to come from the tension between these two poles. " If I recognise all my misery, then I am bound to depend on Him

[1] *De spiritu et anima*, 50.

through Whom I am . . . without Whom I can do nothing." With the object of forcing this tension to its highest point every energy was given to portraying the misery of human nature as clearly as possible and to encouraging contempt, disgust, and even hatred of one's own self and of the whole world. Eternal blessedness was compared with earthly misery so as to arouse this wished-for feeling of disgust. " This life revolts me exceedingly." Meditation turned on the opposition between God and man : " Thou art in heaven, I on earth. Thou lovest the highest, I the lowest. . . . Thou art good, I evil ; Thou holy, I contemptible. Thou art the light, I am blind ; Thou art life, I am death". And the result of this self-contemplation is : " Woe is me. . . . I am a putrefying corpse, the food for worms, a dirty vessel, the food for fire ". "What am I—a dark abyss, a land of misery, a son of passion, a vessel of ignominy. Begot in impurity, I live in misery and will die in agony. Alas, wretched that I am, what am I, what will I be ? Yes, what am I ? A dung-heap, a vessel of corruption, full of filth and frightfulness." [1]

We meet this attitude also in the *Imitation of Christ*. " Who am I ", prays the writer, " that I should dare to talk to Thee, my Lord and God ? I am Thy poorest servant, a prostrate worm, much poorer and more wretched than I know. Remember, O Lord, that I am nothing, have nothing, and can do nothing." The writer exhorts repeatedly : " consider thy sins with great displeasure and affliction. Do not esteem thyself for something because of thy good works. Thou art in truth a sinner enslaved and entangled in many passions. From

---

[1] *Meditationes piissimae de cognitione humanae conditionis* (falsely ascribed to St. Bernard).

thy very nature thou strivest always towards nothingness. Thou fallest quickly, quickly art thou overcome, quickly confounded, quickly deprived of strength. Thou hast nothing for which thou couldst extol thyself, but much for which thou must esteem thyself as worthless. Thou art far weaker than thou canst understand. Do not, therefore, consider as great what thou dost. Do not make the appearance of being elevated, of being valuable, worth admiring, worth recognition ". " Learn to obey, thou dust . . . learn to humble thyself, thou earth and mud . . . and to bend under every foot. Show thyself small and submissive so that all could tread on you and trample you like mud in the streets . . . thou creature of nothingness . . . thou impure sinner."

It must be conceded that the author clearly emphasises that God is the source of all good in man. The very recognition of one's own weakness and the contrition resulting from it should decide God to vouchsafe the help of His grace. " If I hold myself for worthless and make myself nothing . . . if I refrain from all self-esteem and make myself dust . . . then Thy grace will succour me and Thy light will be near my heart. . . . If Thou gazest once upon me, straightway I become strong and filled with new joy." Certainly the theory of both the aspects of Christian consciousness are correctly understood, but there is so much talk of the negative side that it is bound to make the reader see nothing but that. And this is what the authors wished. Humility, not love, was the pivot of their religious system. For that very reason they devoted all their energy to trying to present man's defects and sinfulness, the foundation of humility. Unfortunately in doing this they neglected to describe in sufficient detail the divine gifts of God and the Christian confidence of which they are the basis. Thus the fine balance between humility and confidence was destroyed, and from the one-sided over-emphasis of humility there was bound to result a stunting of the Christian consciousness and the confidence which is based on God.

The consequences were obvious. The exaggerated cultivation of the sense of sin nullified religious joy. Of course the authors referred to the " eternal consolations " which " are only given to those who shun the consolations of this world ". Of course they praised in terms of deep experience the sweetness felt by the soul when mystically enwrapped in God here below. But how many readers could attain such summits ? To the majority this joyful experience was absolutely closed.

The result of the artificial suppression of confidence was the complete lack of an ambitious spirit of enterprise in working for the Kingdom of God, both in the individual soul and in the surrounding world. The writer of the *Imitation of Christ* obviously suffered for this : " Often it is some small thing that afflicts and oppresses me. I intend to act decidedly but there comes a small temptation and I feel very fearful. Often it is quite a small thing, but a great temptation rises out of it. And if I feel only slightly sure—so slightly that I scarcely even notice it— then often I find myself overcome by only a breath." There is even greater fear in the lamentation of the soliloquy : " one moment I am happy and straightway I am sad. One moment I feel strength and then straightway weakness. Now I live and then straightway I am dead . . . so change underlies all, and scarcely for an hour do I remain in the same condition . . . see, O lord, how great is the misery of man in which I find myself ". Of course the authors exhorted against such lack of courage : " You ought not to let yourself be alienated and straightway overwhelmed when you hear of the way of perfection ; you should rather feel yourself urged on to higher things." But how can a soul find courage to climb joyously upwards when it is preached at continuously to be " always mindful of its own evil and nothingness ! " From the trust in God's help ? The authors expatiate on this clearly enough. But the funda mental maxim remains unshaken : " grace builds on nature ". And the laws of psychology teach us that joyful and courageous thoughts have a very weak echo in hearts that are weighed down with dismal and oppressed feelings.

We are warned of this by a glance at life and history. We observe that people make up for the lack of joy in religion by means of earthly substitutes. Earthly satisfaction takes the place of heavenly joy. They abandon the cultivation of the inner man and concentrate their soul's energy on the outer activities of their business or profession. The ideal of accomplishment takes the place of development of personality, and then the will to success takes the place of the ideal of accomplishment.

The consequences can be most clearly seen in their extreme heretical form. It is no coincidence that the pessimistic religious systems of Calvinism and English Puritanism in the Seventeenth and Eighteenth Centuries made a fruitful pasture for rising Capitalism. Business honesty became a virtue and economic success its reward. In the hey-day of Capitalist economics people were ready to expatiate on the superiority of Protestant countries over Catholic ones. To-day, when the ruinous results of this attitude are spread before us, these songs of praise have been silenced. But to-day too we suffer from a certain secularisation of joy and an over-estimation of trivial accomplishments at the expense of personality.

It would be thoroughly false to say that this pessimism was the outcome of the " Dark Middle Ages ", as is said so readily. The Middle Ages had a real and deep joy in God. Even to-day we stand amazed before what they achieved. It would be folly, too, to blame the one-sided and insufficient character of a few books, as though they were the teaching of the Catholic Church. The foremost theologians, distinguished by the Church with the title of *Doctor Ecclesiæ*, have declared that a really Christian consciousness contains both virtues—humility and confidence. In spite of his pessimism, St. Augustine wrote that " It is good to have confidence, but not for oneself, which is pride, but for God ". And St. Thomas Aquinas, the greatest moral theologian of the Middle Ages, whose work forms the basis of every text-book of moral theology even to-day, turns indignantly on those who do not wish to recognise the good they obtain from God. " That is not humility, but ungratefulness." The expression of the psalmist applies to such people : " And man when he was in honour did not understand ; he is compared to senseless beasts, and is become like to them ". We always should and we always need to turn our gaze on the gifts God has bestowed on us. For it is the consideration of God's goodness and charity which " awakens love " and " strengthens devotion ".

St. Teresa of Avila shares this view. The stark pessimism of the *Imitation of Christ* and similar ideas had been echoed powerfully in Spanish literature. But St. Teresa saw the danger of discouragement which is bound to come from this attitude. " If we never get away from the swamp of our misery," she writes, " we will suffer great damage. . . . A thousand thoughts upset the soul and lead it astray. . . . For example, dare I risk to undertake this or that ? Is it not arrogance for such a miserable creature as I to be busied about something so noble as interior prayer ? " Teresa herself had experienced similar temptations, and observed the same questionings in others. " These souls never stop contemplating their own misery and they think it is pure humility."

But really there is a deception waiting to trap them. With such people it is the devil who " turns their knowledge of self to their own undoing ". " He produces a false idea of humility in them, with which they make little progress." He makes it look like pride to imitate the saints and entertain high, inordinate desires. " What harm the devil has caused to many souls," complains the saint, " through insinuating such thoughts ! "

And further on she lays blame on " certain temptations which conceal themselves under the appearance of humility ". " Many people think it is humility not to recognise the gifts God has bestowed on them. . . . Of course God bestows the gifts without our meriting them. But we must be thankful to His majesty for them. For if we do not recognise what we have received from Him, we will not awaken to His love." It is clear that the more we love somebody who has proved his charity to us, the more we think of his charity. " It is quite certain that we obtain so much more, and are richer, with the recognition of our own poverty. For in this way humility is immediately increased. But if, as soon as God begins to share great bounties with it, the soul draws back because it does not think itself capable of them, the soul is merely discouraged." " Therefore I repeat again and again, that if our Lord shows His grace to you, and gives you

opportunity to undertake some work or other for His
sake, do not be held back from that by the thought that
you are sinners. Faith must win the victory over our
wretchedness . . . the sight of the weakness of our flesh
ought not to discourage us. . . . We must trust in His
compassion, but entirely mistrust our own strength."

St. Teresa asks for the cultivation of both aspects of
Christian self-awareness, humility because of our human
weakness, and confidence because of divine grace. In
her opinion God lets us know the graces received for this
very reason, so that we grow stronger in belief, and
humble. "According to my judgment", she declares,
"it is impossible to undertake great things courageously
with our nature as it is constituted, unless we realise that
we are in God's grace." And this knowledge, far from
endangering, increases humility, for by the contrast
between the black and the white, the white appears more
resplendent, and the black more dismal. Of herself the
saint confesses that in good actions she "usually does
not think at all of herself, but straightway praises God",
for "all the good that we do comes not in its origin from
us but from that Spring by which the tree of our soul is
planted, from that Sun which bestows warmth on our
works".

And St. Francis de Sales, whose eyes are always turned
to God's love for man, is incapable of not seeing the
divine illumination in the soul. Francis knew the teaching of Aquinas, and made it the basis of his own work.
He deals twice with the question we are discussing, once
in the *Introduction*, and once in a piece of direction given
to his nuns. "These two virtues, humility and confidence," he affirms very clearly, "are so deeply bound
up with one another that they are never separated and

cannot subsist apart." Hence it is impossible to conceive the nature of confidence rightly without understanding humility and *vice versa*. In common with Aquinas, Francis sharply criticises that " false and stupid humility " which refuses to see the personal advantages bestowed on us by God. To proceed in this way means committing " a serious wrong " against God, " because God's gifts should be recognised, treasured highly, and held in high esteem ". The ancient philosophers said " know thyself ", and " all true Christians " are in agreement with them. This self-knowledge should by no means be limited to the knowledge of our meanness and weakness. That would give us a false picture. " Let each man recognise his natural assets," exhorted St. Ambrose. " Let him know the goodness he possesses, but let him also be aware of his faults." This is Francis's opinion. We should " know the excellence and great value of our soul, which is capable of union with the divine goodness ". Of course we must always remember that all the great things worked in us by God are not of our own meriting. " But because we possess them we should also rejoice in them, while praising God alone, because He is the author of them." Francis takes as example the *Magnificat* of Our Lady. As humble handmaid of the Lord she knows her abjectness, and yet she recognises triumphantly that all generations must call her blessed. And he refers to St. Paul who describes himself humbly as " the least amongst the saints ", and yet dares to make the bold assertion : " I can do all things in Him Who strengtheneth me ".

We should not reject the knowledge of the good in us, but only reject the denial that we owe it to God. Mary's soul was completely sunk in God, and she recognised, joyfully, the work God performed in her. But the heart of the Pharisee in the Temple was only filled with egotism, and his prayer itself became for him the clothing of his conceit. Pelagius, who denied original sin and defended the theory of man's absolute sinlessness through his own strength alone, once composed a prayer for the widow Juliana, which serves as a universal example of pharisaical self-righteousness. " Thou knowest O Lord how guiltless are these hands I raise to Thee, how pure they are from all deceit and unrighteousness. Thou knowest how righteous and spotless and free from all deceit are these lips with which I pray your pity." If we compare this prayer with the *Magnificat* the profound difference is clearly noticeable. In Pelagius' prayer we find self-admiration remote from God, which springs from the conviction of his own excellence. In the *Magnificat* there is unselfish praise of almighty God Who gave such great gifts through His love. These two prayers are as different from one another as their two sources, one a theocentric, and the other an egocentric, condition of spirit.

St. Francis de Sales wishes to make us aware of God's gifts, and to instil in us a grateful admiration for the good which blooms in our souls under the breath of the Holy Ghost. We should look joyfully into the secret Paradise which Our Lord has created in our hearts. Then we will learn to pray with our ever blessed Lady : " My soul doth magnify the Lord, for the Almighty God has worked great things in me." It is our duty to do this, and the Church herself directs us to it when she puts the *Magnificat* into the mouth of her priests every day at Vespers. Francis wants to beget and preserve the spirit of the *Magnificat* in the Christian soul, the spirit of a joyous love of God. And it is for this reason that he recommends us to consider attentively the graces we have received. For, as St.

Thomas said, the consideration of God's grace is the best means of kindling love for the Bestower. Francis even goes further. With his sensitiveness as spiritual director he noticed that every man sets a higher worth on his individual benefits than he sets on benefits he has in common with others. So he said that " these special gifts must be considered with special attention ", for in this way we are provided with a powerful encouragement to love God. Other writers may immediately scent the danger lying here of vain self-complacency, and, like St. Bernard, recommend us to look only at our faults and not our advantages. But Francis rejects such pessimism and timidity. " In this they are certainly deceived. There is no need to fear that the knowledge of the things that God has worked in us will make us puffed up, if only we keep mindful that all the good in us does not spring from us."

On this point there is a cleavage between Francis's view and the opinion of other doctors of the spiritual life, especially the school of the *Imitation of Christ*. The basis of the difference lies in the difference of the part played by love in the religious system. For Francis love is the beginning and end of all high moral development, and the centre and heart of religious life. Therefore he is not prepared to abandon a means so fitted for developing our joyful love of God, because of some small possible danger. With other writers, for instance St. Bernard, and the Fathers of the Desert in the Fourth Century, the central position occupied by love in the religious life is not so clearly realised.

Besides love, humility takes a prominent place as the kernel of all virtues. The figure of the tree of life and death, which became so popular after the Twelfth

Century, made the tree of vice grow up out of the seed of pride, and the tree of virtue out of humility. This idea is contained in Christ's first precept : Humility of heart is the foundation of all virtue. It is necessary for achieving eternal salvation. Though he recognised that a humble disposition is the basis of a correct approach to God, even here Francis wrote the word " love " instead of the word " humility ". Obviously the other writers we have been discussing conceived of " love " as the " bond of perfection ". But humility prepared the way to perfection. Consequently self-judgment had resulted in self-contempt. But Francis conceives of love not only as the definition of perfection but also as the way leading to it, the means to it. We will go into this later. But anyhow, this love is inflamed by the knowledge of the advantage God has bestowed on one. Hence St. Francis de Sales enjoins a joyful and grateful consideration on our part of our own worth.

Francis expects this mode of procedure to have two results. First of all, astounding though it may seem, he expects a deepening of our humility. Nothing can make a noble soul conscious of the unworthiness of the smallest sin so much as considering the graces it has received. In the shining light of divine love the smallest weakness seems unspeakably hateful, and laziness, which infringes no commandment, looks shamefully mean. As a second result, Francis expects a growth of activity. He knows that self-contempt means self-abandonment. Taken by themselves, humility, and an awareness of guilt and weakness, are bound to lead to a lack of courage—we have already seen how this danger threatened the *Imitation of Christ* group—and a resignation of hope of high development. It can cloak weakness, timidity, and a lazy comfort. This danger has also been revealed by modern psychology, but Francis had already seen it. According to him, the representatives of false humility say that " they leave interior prayer to the perfect, because they themselves are not worthy of it, and rarely dare to go to Holy Communion because they do not feel pure enough ". They shelter behind their unworthiness, and bury the talent bestowed on them by God. Francis tore away the veil covering this sort of humble conduct which interferes with one's end. He unmasked it for what it really was, self-deception, and deception of others. This false " bad humility is nothing else than a subterfuge hiding the wish to follow one's own opinion and to yield to the propensity to indolence ". True humility says : " I can do nothing, and I am not so much as pure nothingness ". But then true humility returns to confidence which says : " There is nothing and can be nothing that I could not do, if only I set all my trust in God who can do all things ".

As a good psychologist Francis had noticed that one's energy is strengthened by positive affections, and weakened by negative ones. In his capacity as spiritual director he purposely placed his optimistic conception of man at the centre of his ascetical theory. In the first consideration laying the foundation for a religious life he says to *Philothea :* " God hath drawn thee out of nothingness so as to make of thee what thou art. . . . Thou art the first amongst all beings of the visible world ". He puts in the mouth of the soul, by way of answer to this consideration : " I will follow my Creator, and feel myself honoured in the being which He gave me ". And at the conclusion of this book, which he used to lay in the hands of all who entrusted themselves to his direction, he mentions five considerations for the strengthening of religious life. The first is called : " Concerning the nobleness of the human soul ". It begins " *Consideres la noblesse et l'Excellence de vostre âme* ". " How lofty is our heart." " O thou, my beautiful soul ", cries the saint in wonder.[1]

What a noble thought there is in the beauty of the soul ! It was conceived, first of all, by Plato. Plato describes virtue as the harmony of the forces of the soul, and with that he introduced the æsthetic train into ethical ideas. The *Kallokagathia* became an ideal of the Greeks, and the very word signifies the combination of the concepts beautiful and good. The Fathers of the Church, who were more deeply versed in Plato's idealistic flight of thought than in the more temperate ideas of Aristotle, joyfully took over this conception. " Beauty of soul . . . has something wonderful in it," wrote Clement of Alexandria. And the Milanese prince of the Church who was the first to force an Emperor to do ecclesiastical penance, St. Ambrose, speaks tenderly and poetically of " the graceful charm of the soul that believes ", and the " virgin beauty of the blameless soul ". " Know thyself, O noble soul ", he exhorts, " Thou art the image of God. Know thyself, O man, for thou art God's glory ". He turns his gaze joyfully upon himself and then prays gratefully to God. " When I contemplate myself . . . the secrets of Thy being are revealed to me. How wonderfully thy greatness beams in my creaturely self ! " According to St. Augustine " each soul is beautiful, not through itself, but through the light of God which it shares ". " Thou art beautiful, my friend ", says the *Song of Songs*, and Ambrose declared that the beauty of the soul is intended here. The bride's beauty in the

[1] *Œuvres*, Vol. III, pp. 34 *sq*.

Song of Songs gave subsequent writers occasion to speak repeatedly of the beauty of the soul. St. Thomas and other scholastics set forth the outline of spiritual beauty.

With Sixteenth Century Spanish mysticism these ideas bloomed afresh. Praise of beauty of soul resounds in St. Teresa and Gracian, her spiritual advisor. John of Avila in his description is at one with St. Thomas, without however indicating his source. There was a cult of the *alma bella*, the beautiful soul, and holiness and humanism were joyously wedded. " The divine and beautiful soul is married with a divine and beautiful body by the Creator ", wrote Louis Richeome. Francis adopts this enthusiasm, which is so congenial to him. " *O ma belle âme* ", " O my little lovely soul, thou that canst know and love God, why dost thou take delight in trivial things. Thou hast an eternity to struggle for, so why dost thou want to delight in a moment ? "

(c) *Religious Significance of Joy*

As a result of his optimistic conception of God and Man, there is a quiet joyfulness in Francis's soul. His religious spirit sparkles with supernatural joy, and the reflection of this extends to the temporal order, too. Often a fine humour is revealed in his words. " Joy is the strong feather in eternal nature ", says Schiller, and Francis is representative of a viewpoint similar but springing from a theocentric conception of the world. His knowledge of psychology and education makes him want the religious individual always to preserve his joyful state. The harmful influence of emotional depression on the religious life had been recognised by Egyptian monasticism in the Fourth Century. To the Fathers of the Desert sadness seemed as sure a sign of the presence of evil spirits as joy of the presence of good spirits. When a list of principal sins began to be assembled, not seven were counted—according to our custom—but eight. The eighth was sadness. Cassian introduced this doctrine into the West. It was taken over by the early mediæval penitential books and the sinner who had given in to sad or depressed feelings was given penances like those for avarice or sloth. Gregory the Great reduced the eight capital sins to seven because of his preference for the number seven. He merged sadness and sloth together on account of their near relationship and described the vice as sadness. It has only been called sloth since St. Thomas Aquinas. And so it happened that ascetical writers of a later date, though always hinting at sloth in spiritual life, did not sufficiently emphasise the importance of religious joy and the serious harm done by a melancholy attitude to religious development. Occasional hints about joy were not able to undo this harm.

It is Francis de Sales's merit that he broke new ground in the idea of religious joy. The Italian school of the Sixteenth Century had prepared the way for him.[1] But he brings into full daylight the joyful character of Catholic devotion. He preaches with emphasis that the preservation of a joyful temperament is a moral duty and denounces sadness as an " exceptionally dangerous " condition. He devoted a number of long discussions, principally a special chapter in the *Introduction*, to the inquiry into this evil and the struggle against it. In the *Introduction* he describes exactly the serious psychological disturbances which result from this condition of feeling. " It upsets the soul, bringing disorder and unrest. It

---

[1] Pourrat, *op. cit.*, Vol. III, pp. 349 *sq.*

arouses unfounded fears and robs prayer of its savour. The head becomes heavy and sleepy and the spirit, without counsel and clear judgment, loses courage and its strength is cast down. In short it is like a hard winter which oppresses all the beauty of the earth and numbs the animals with cold. For it steals all joy from the mind and makes the soul lame and powerless in all its forces." " Joy opens the heart and sadness shuts it ", declares Francis later in the *Traitté*, and he shows by use of psychological observation as well as some examples taken from literature that joy gives one a certain desirableness to the beloved object whereas sadness obstructs one's access to uplifting influences. Francis, like Cassian and the whole of moral theology in the early Middle Ages, gives a list of other moral failings resulting from the fundamental failing of sadness. The Middle Ages saw " fear, sloth, unreadiness, jealousy, envy and impatience " as the offspring of sadness. Holy Scripture rightly declares that " depression has killed many and brings no value ".[1]

Towards the end of the *Traitté* a whole chapter is devoted to showing that " sadness is always unprofitable and in contradiction to the service of God ". The saint also mentions three causes for depressed spirits : " Frequently they come from the devil who, with a thousand sad, melancholy and annoying insinuations, depresses the judgment of the understanding, weakens the strength of the will, and disrupts the whole soul. Just as a thick cloud fills one's head and breast with vapours, making breathing difficult and confusing one, so the devil fills the soul of man with sad thoughts, deprives him of the faculty of raising his heart to God, makes him somnolent

[1] *Œuvres*, Vol. III, pp. 311, 314.

and discouraged to an extreme degree so as to bring him to doubt and ruin." Once again Francis takes an example from Pliny's *Natural History* of which he was so fond. There is a fish called muddy-fish or sea-devil which stirs up the mud of the sea and lies in wait in the troubled waters for unsuspecting fry. " Perhaps from this the expression of ' fishing in troubled waters ' is derived." " The devil of hell acts in a similar way." After he has confused the understanding and led it astray, he makes an unsuspected attack on the life of the emotions. " He overwhelms them with doubts, with feelings of aversion and jealousy, with groundless fears over past sins, and with so many trivial, bitter and melancholy fantasies that the soul turns away from all reason and consolation."

A second cause of sadness lies in a melancholy temperament. This is a natural disposition and therefore no moral fault is entailed. But it gives the devil a handle for enslaving our souls with a thousand temptations. In cloudy weather, the saint remarked, flies drop most easily into the spider's web.

The third cause, according to Francis, comes merely from the rebuffs of fate. These come to good and bad people equally and both good and bad suffer natural pain. But while religious people, through their bond with God, can limit or dispel the unavoidable influence of the outer world on their feelings, weak characters surrender to unrestrained joy and unrestrained pain. Again there is a comparison taken from natural history, this time a very powerful one : " These people are like monkeys and marmots which, when the moon wanes, are in a melancholy and depressed mood, but when it waxes they frisk about and dance and make buffooneries ".[1] This is

_____
[1] *Œuvres*, Vol. V, pp. 315 *sq.*

strongly put for a kindly saint like Francis and therefore all the more worth noticing. It shows his desire to uproot irresoluteness and moodiness from our feelings.

Whatever its cause, sadness is always very deterimental to the development of a true religious spirit. In fact human sadness is a source of pleasure for the devil. The devil presents evil in an enticing guise and he twists the good into repulsive shapes. Since he is trying to make the sinner revel in his evil, he tries to make him forget that his holy life ever caused him joy. Condemned to eternal misery himself, the devil tries to entrap mankind into the same fate, and misery and melancholy give the very opportunity he desires to drive goodness out of the soul.

If we compare this doctrine with that of St. Francis of Assisi, we observe how much both saints agree on the part played by joy and sadness in religion. " The saint," says Thomas of Cellano, referring to St. Francis of Assisi, " affirmed that spiritual joy was the surest defence against the thousand traps of the devil." " For the devil rejoices most if he can rob a servant of God of spiritual joy. For, as long as the heart is filled with spiritual joy, the serpent's sting is impotent. The demons can do nothing with a servant of Christ if they see him filled with holy joy. But if the soul is cast down, dejected and depressed, it is easily gripped by sadness and thus turns towards frivolity."

These last words reveal a great danger which appears in times of unconsoled pain. The desire for life revolts against the unbearable tension, and we try at all costs to escape from boredom. We seize hold of any means at our disposal to distract us, and hurl ourselves into the turmoil of sensual pleasure. Later, disillusioned and stained with sin, we awaken to a misery greater than the first.

Therefore there should be no room for sadness. Even when we observe our imperfections, the slowness of our progress, even our regress in the spiritual life, St. Francis de Sales does not want us to give way to *ennui*, depression and sadness. To do this would only be to add another fault to the one already there. Irritation and vexation with oneself " comes in no way from the proper motives of the virtue of penitence, but from the embryonic self-love in our nature ".[1] If the soul is really " a child in humility . . . it will not be surprised if it falls once . . . " God Himself is not astounded or angry at our misfortune because He knows how weak we are. " Our Lord looks down from the summit of heaven " on the soul, " as a father looks on his child which is still weak and finds it hard to keep on its feet. Come on a little, my child, he says, and if it falls he urges it to take heart . . . do not cry ! . . . and he reaches it his hand." When Christ was born the angels sang " Peace to men of good-will ". To receive the child Jesus into our hearts it is enough to be of good-will, for Jesus has come to bless our good-will and He will make it fruitful, little by little, if only we let ourselves be led by Him. Francis wrote to the Abbess of Puits d'Orbe : " Only return to the good as soon as you notice you have strayed from it. Remain true to this and you will always live really happily ".[2]

So sadness is never justified on whatever ground it may try to base itself, and it is always a moral duty to oppose it. The struggle will lead to victory only if the will is fully determined " to overcome moods and inclinations " and to have recourse to the means of salvation corresponding to its needs.

---

[1] *Œuvres*, Vol. III, p. 345.
[2] *Œuvres*, Vol. XIX, pp. 196, 91 *sq.* ; Vol. XIV, p. 146.

Principiis obsta was the ancient adage. " Beware of all sad and melancholy thoughts " is the advice of the saint. To turn immediately and calmly to God is the best way of stifling melancholy. One should not probe one's depression and allow the imagination to dwell on it, because usually it is worse in the imagination than in the fact.

To-day people are always asking how it is possible to stifle the thoughts which spring to the mind unconsciously. Of course it is impossible to hinder their coming, but as soon as their presence is observed the soul should drive them out with a positive act of will. Francis has not gone into the details of this, but experience seems to show that it is worth keeping to a definite method. For instance one can make use of certain imperatives such as " Stop ", " Begone " or " Finish ". In this way the dangerous current of thought can be stemmed instantaneously, and later even automatically.

But if sadness cannot be dispelled in this way then it must be fought systematically. If its cause is physical or psychological, one should go to a doctor and carry out his advice scrupulously. Moreover, sadness's opposing emotions—confidence in God and love—must be carefully cultivated. St. James says : " Is anyone sad amongst you, so let him pray". The prayers prayed should naturally be so chosen as to give no outlet for melancholy. Once Francis was asked whether we should talk to God about our cares and our miseries or rather talk to Him of other things. His wise answer was : " It is better to turn our soul away from its sadness when we speak with God, and let it dwell on other things, not on pain . . . because this will only remind us of our pain anew ".[1] The prayers

[1] *Œuvres*, Vol. VI, p. 84.

should be chosen so as to " lead to confidence and love of God ". Francis mentions as examples short ejaculations such as : " My beloved God, my kindest Redeemer ! God of my heart, my joy, my hope, dearest most beloved bridegroom of my soul ! " " O Jesus be my Jesus, and my soul will live."

Modern psychology has established that an idea has more influence on the spirit the more man's other forces are put into its service. Francis was quite conscious of this and recommended that prayers should be spoken out loud. He makes reference to the importance of singing hymns and recommends the use of physical gestures in order to increase one's fervour. " Press the crucifix to thy heart. Kiss the feet of the Crucified."

A second remedy that goes hand in hand with this method consists of withdrawing psychical energy from sad thoughts. If this is done they crumple up of themselves. The charmed circle of sadness is broken immediately by a humble and frank discussion with a spiritual director about " all those experiences, feelings and ideas ". " So as to divert the soul from its sad thoughts ", one should " busy oneself with every sort of external work ". One " should seek as much as possible the conversation of religious persons " and, finally, the best of all means consists in the knowledge that all the incidents of this life are unimportant trivialities compared with the immeasurable blessedness of the other life, and then one should let the will soar upwards into union with the will of God. If the soul achieves this highest love of God, then naturally the tension between the evil and the will which is fighting the evil will disappear and the psychological cause of all sad and melancholy thoughts will be removed. " As soon as one is quite determined to accept the cross that God lays on us, it is no longer a cross . . . it is a cross only because we do not want it . . . but if it comes from God how can we not want it ? " [1]

Thus Francis uses the same methods that a modern nerve specialist would use in a case of psychical depression. The only difference would be about the value of a further effort to divert melancholy which Francis mentions, namely, " discreet use of the scourge ". He adds as confirmation that " outer chastisement brings inner consolations and with the experience of the external pain the soul turns away from its inner pain ". We first come across the " discipline " in religious history as a form of punishment in the cloister ; subsequently it made its way into the system of penitential discipline and in the Eleventh Century Peter Damien advised voluntary scourging. The main motive seems to have been the desire to be like the suffering Saviour, the desire for a substitute for longed-for martyrdom, and the hope of doing penance for sins and of gaining merit for heaven. Scourging became popular as a means of asceticism under the influence of St. Peter Damien and St. Antony of Padua, and it was also used as a penance for the capital sin of sadness. For this sin the penitential books had prescribed : " fasting on bread and water ", and cutting out all conversation with others until the sinner came back " with serenest face and joyous heart ". The early Middle Ages had not sufficiently recognised the psychological and physiological causes of sadness, and this was due to the unfortunate association with sloth that it had at that time. The means suitable for dealing with sloth are in no way suitable for dealing with sadness. St.

[1] *Œuvres*, Vol. III, pp. 314–316.

Thomas called attention to the fact that "physical weakness disposed one to sadness". St. Francis de Sales did not follow the tradition of recommending fasting as a punishment for depression, and he went directly contrary to his forerunners in advising "frequent conversation" for such cases. Scourging he held as profitable, but in a letter of the year 1604 he remarks that "this means should be used only with great moderation and only in so far as the experience of a few days proves it to be useful". At a later age he opposed all forms of harsh punishment. Hence there is reason to call into question the value of scourging as a means of distraction. On the other hand it is tenable that this summoning-up of the whole strength of the will, which is an essential element in self-chastisement, can break through the dusk of slight cases of spiritual depression. Francis appears to have this possibility in mind when he says that "scourging has a remarkable power for awakening religious efforts". But the good effect must be obvious after a few attempts ; Francis thoroughly opposes a fruitless and often harmful extension of scourging. However this may be it is certain that he wished to leave no means untried, and he did not shrink from severe measures when it was a question of banishing depression from religious life.

The way to perfection is a long one and only a joyous temperament can pursue it. Just as a plant turns to the light and is spoilt by shadow, so the sunlight of joy is necessary for the soul's development. The generations that followed had a clear understanding of the joyful character of Salesian devotion. The year 1653 saw the appearance in Paris of the *Introduction* in verse. The versifier gives a faithful rendering of Francis's description of the religious attitude of the period.

> *Ainsi selon sa passion*
> *De l'interest tousiours guidée*
> *Chaqu'un paient la dévotion*
> *Triste, rude, vaine ou fardée.*

(Everybody depicts religion as sad, crude, indifferent, or pompous, according to his own pattern and always guided by his own interest.)

This caricature, he says, results in a general contempt of religion :

> *Tout le monde aujourd'huy la banit de son cœur*
> *Parce qu'on la depient d'une noire couleur.*
> *Et que ces gens noyez dans l'abysme des vices*
> *Disent, quelle est chagrine, et quelle a de caprices*
> *Et qu'elle oste la joye aux conversations*
> *Par sa melancholie et ses corrections.*[1]

(To-day everybody banishes it from his heart because it is described in such black colours, and because people who are drowned in the abyss of vice say it is sad and freakish, and that it takes away joy from social life by its melancholy and its admonitions.)

The religion of St. Francis de Sales is anything but sombre. In fact he could almost be compared to the laughing and friendly madonnas of the Middle Ages. " God is the God of joy ", writes the saint ; " the spirit of joy is the true spirit of devotion ". In a sermon he once declared : " If you have a sorrowful face at the conclusion of your prayers it is a clear sign that you have not prayed as you ought to have done ".[2] We ought to

---

[1] *Introduction à la vie dévote en vers françois par le Sieur N.H.E. S.D.M.* . . . (Paris, 1653), pp. 2, 8.
[2] *Œuvres*, Vol. XIII, pp. 16, 112.

G 2

wend our way towards God with joy. " The righteous man hath joy in the Lord ", says the Psalmist, and St. Paul advises us to " rejoice in the Lord at all times, and again I say rejoice ". " What is commanded," asked St. Augustine, and answers : " that we should rejoice in the Lord." " I cannot understand ", says Francis, " how souls that have given themselves to divine goodness can ever fail to be joyful ; for is there any happiness like this " ? " I cannot conceive how you can let your heart be filled with such deep sorrow, considering you are a child of God, entrusted to His lovingkindness, and consecrated to His love." " What happiness comes from belonging entirely to God ! He loves His own, He protects them and accompanies them to the blessed haven of their desires." " Therefore do not let your soul be depressed, nor live in spiritual bitterness. For He Who has loved you so much and Who died that you might live, is so good, so loving and so worthy of love." St. Philip Neri used to say : " Be joyful, my children." In Francis's books and letters we frequently come across the admonishment : " Be joyful ", " *Vives joyeuse en Dieu*," " *Soyes joyeusement dévote*," " *Vives saintement joyeuse*," " Live joyfully ! Our Lord is looking down on you lovingly." [1] Holy joy, or, as we should say, joyful holiness would be a good motto for our time.

St. Paul writes : " The fruit of the Holy Ghost is . . . joy and peace ". Psychologically these two belong to one another. Seen from the point of view of religious development they are the pillars of a true and successful devotion. It is for this reason that Francis holds the cultivation of inner joy and the preservation of spiritual peace in such high esteem. The Jesuit, Father Mugnier, followed him

[1] *Œuvres*, Vol. XIII, p. 47.

in 1647 by championing the thesis that Christian perfection is of a joyful nature. His fellow-Jesuit, P. le Moyne, got the ideas of his book called *Joyful Religion*, which was published in 1652, out of the Salesian inheritance. To Pascal and the Jansenists it was a bone of contention. The Salesian spirit breathes through the pages of Lombez's (died 1778) *Concerning Joy in the Soul*. " Joy is one of the fruits of the Holy Ghost. The fulness of the Holy Ghost which fashions the saints involves the fulness of joy. To this fulness are we exhorted by the apostle whom Christ loved. All other apostles give us the same advice and their epistles breed the spirit of holy joy." [1] On the threshold of this painful century of ours, Bishop von Keppler cried out : " More joy ". Recognising the sickness and difficulties of the age, he wrote a little book on joy in God. He will always be reckoned among the greatest advocates of joy in religion. The basis of his work is set out in the noble declaration : " Joy is a factor in life, a need of life, a strength in life, and a value of life ". He refers to a traditional anecdote about St. Francis de Sales which gives a good idea of the saint's attitude. Somebody once told him of a man who led a saintly life but who nevertheless always looked sorrowful. To this Francis replied : " If a saint were sorry, he would be a sorry saint ".

(ii) PERSONAL LIFE AND SOCIAL POSITION

(a) The " Individual Ideal of Perfection "

" God created man after His image and likeness." The most perfect man is the man in whom this likeness

---

[1] Pourrat, *op. cit.*, Vol. IV, p. 364.

is implanted most deeply. Hence the objective proto-type for man is the absolute perfection of God Who, as Being itself, realises infinitely the idea of the true, the good and the beautiful from whom everything that is true, good and beautiful derives. All human perfection lies in union with this divine original perfection. There-fore Christ says : " Be perfect as your Father in Heaven is perfect ".

Now it is quite impossible for God's infinity to be perfectly reflected in the finiteness of human nature. The image of the original can be reflected in each man only within the limits of his personality. The extent of different personal capabilities varies with individuals. Though God made all men after His image and likeness, He did not make them all like one another ; He formed each one unique and individual in kind. Cicero, at the conclusion of his *Panætius*, opposed the Stoa's tendency to standardise humanity, with the declaration that " by nature we are endowed with a kind of double personality —the first is common to all human beings, the possession of reason . . . the second is particular and is bestowed on each individual man for himself. Just as there are great differences in bodies . . . so between souls there are still greater differences ". St. Thomas Aquinas taught that individual differences were the result of man's physical nature and the association of the soul with the body, a very modern if also much debated conception. No soul, he declared, could go into another body as it goes into its own.

As a consequence of the differences in our spiritual and physical make-up, the objective model appears different to different people. We have already seen that there are two outlooks on God—even within the strict field of orthodoxy—that which emphasises His omnipotence and justice, and that which emphasises His goodness and love. Thus the Divine Image of perfection varies according to the different temperaments, inclinations, faults and weaknesses of every person. Everyone is different, too, in the externals of life—such as are effected by birth, family, one's milieu, and the spiritual and material means at one's disposal. In course of time, the necessities of life and the spirit of the age, indifferent to other ideas, imprint their traces on the soul's development. According to the will of God the objective ideal—that is to say, the pure reflection of divine perfection—has to be re-valued according to the individual ideal. By " individual ideal ", is meant the creation of the greatest possible resemblance of a given individual with the Divine Prototype. My general desire to be perfect like our Father in heaven becomes transformed into the practical decision to form in myself the image that God thought, willed, and loved when He created me. I will realise in myself the ideal personality allotted me by God.

It is important to distinguish clearly between the objective and the subjective ideal. The objective order of values is provided by the closeness or remoteness of one's relationship with God. The highest possible subjective form of development results from a series of conditions, notably the spiritual structure of individual men. Both scales of values can be the same, but they are not bound to be. Thus, for instance, the state of virginity, considered objectively, is higher than that of married life : yet for the majority of men marriage is the highest ideal which God has given them. It would be childish conceit to pretend that the ideal of one's own life is also the highest objective value in the world order. It would be folly and pride for us to deny or revile the real order of creation because what is best for us is not put in the first place. It would be like saying that an expensive ring is worthless because it is too small or too big for our finger. " Will you throw it into the mud if it does not fit your finger ? " asked St. Francis de Sales.[1] We are therefore obliged by faith and reason to see the difference between the objective and the subjective ideals and to form our life according to the image of perfection for which our personality is intended.

The individual ideal is always attainable because it is by God's hand that it is in us. Equally, an effort to go beyond this ideal is bound to be fruitless, and contentment with less would be burying our talent. The only struggle that can be successful is the struggle for our personal ideal of perfection, and this ideal corresponds with the will of the Creator and with that alone.

Unfortunately this truth does not always receive sufficient attention. In the Fourth Century the high enthusiasm for virginity, solitary life, and monasticism caused certain writers and preachers to recommend to everybody the way which, according to Christ, is only accessible to those to whom it is given. This error became more dangerous when people were reckless enough to identify their personal ideal of life with the ideal generally considered to be the highest ; and this, without reference either to their own strength, or to the intendedness on God's side. This error also occurred in early ages. At the period of the persecution of the Church, martyrdom and sanctity were considered synonymous. History therefore showed how people who were not called to martyrdom forced themselves to struggle unnaturally for

[1] *Œuvres*, Vol. V, p. 85.

this crown and subsequently apostatised. In the Fourth
Century Christian asceticism laid special emphasis on
flight from the world and the solitary life in addition to
the renunciation of marriage and possessions ; thus
people who were naturally made for marriage and life in
the world went into the desert. Of course we have no
reason to doubt the purity of the life they chose. But the
great importance given to the struggle against the demon
of unchastity in the admonishments of the Fathers of the
Desert testifies to the difficulties surrounding their
religious development. And history and experience prove
that many people who force themselves into the cloister
or Holy Orders against their natural inclinations end up
outside the Church.

Such efforts to strive after the objectively highest ideal
as opposed to the individual ideal, led, moreover, to
making a substitute-value for the highest good which was
desired but could not be attained. Clement of Alexandria
got a yearning for the martyr's crown and satisfied it with
the idea that the perfect Christian who mortifies himself
in all circumstances is the true martyr. The monks of the
Egyptian desert took over this idea with enthusiasm and
looked on asceticism as a substitute for martyrdom. " The
defence of chastity is also a martyrdom ", says St. Jerome.
Peter Damien based his enthusiasm for scourging on the
same idea. " I would like to endure martyrdom for
Christ, but I have no opportunity . . . therefore I slay
myself with gashes of the scourge and show at least the
desire of my glowing soul." In the Eleventh Century,
when the cloistered life was held in such high esteem, the
laity wanted to die in a religious order even if they had
not lived in one. They made the profession on their
death-beds and were clothed with a habit. Even people

whose lives could hardly be considered to have aimed at personal perfection wanted to be in a condition of perfection when they entered into eternity.

We are shown by history and observation that it is natural to be naïvely envious of the ideal that is objectively the highest. It is natural to hanker after the shining crown of martyrdom, virginity or religious orders. One likes to decorate oneself with it or at least with a substitute for it. But though the great theologians of the Church have always pointed it out, it is often forgotten that God made one man for the monastery and another for the world, and that each man fulfils God's will in the highest degree when he ceaselessly strives to occupy the place allotted him in the vast kingdom of the world.

Few saints have understood the meaning of the individual ideal of perfection with such clarity, or proclaimed it with such energy, as St. Francis de Sales. If Humanism turned people's minds to human personality, Francis, the master of synthesis, knew how to put this way of thinking in the right light—that of the primitive church.

" When God created the world," he says, " He commanded the plants to bear fruit according to their kind. Similarly He commands Christians, who are the living plants of His Church, to bear the fruit of the love, each according to his particular nature and vocation." But people's particular natures are very different. A glance at life shows " that there are no two people who are completely alike as to their natural gifts ". It is the same in the Kingdom of the supernatural. God bestows His graces in immeasurable fulness, but still in such a way " that you never find two people whose supernatural gifts are equal ". " Each person obtains quite special graces."

St. Paul had referred to the variety of the gifts which the
Holy Ghost bestows " as He wishes ". For God never
repeats Himself, but makes each man in a particular way
and for a special form of perfection. " There is a resemblance between all souls which love God in so far as they
give their whole heart to Him with their whole strength.
But they differ in the degree and the form of their dedication to God. One gives himself by martyrdom, another
by virginity, a third through humility, this one in activity,
that one in contemplation, and yet another in the cure of
souls." Though love is the bond of perfection and the
commandment which obliges all similarly, are there
" two souls on earth, two angels in heaven, who ever
possessed complete equality of love ? " Francis is doubtful, and a glance at the legion of saints honoured by the
Church is a corroboration of this doctrine of the individual
stamp of all human perfection. If we compare particular
saints, we get a wonderful diversity of supernatural beauty.
The great holy hermit, St. Paul, for instance, never
practised love of the poor in a way that could be even
compared with St. John, who for that very reason got
the title of " Almsgiver ". Of course every saint has
" all the virtues but not all in the same high degree.
Some saints have been distinguished by one virtue,
others by another. But all obtain blessedness. . . .
There are as many forms of sanctity as there are saints ".[1]
It is unfortunate that when we look at certain pictures of
the saints we get the impression that they all have the
same eyes, the same features, the same posture. And if
one did not hold a sceptre, another a lamb, and a third
a basket of roses one would really not know which was
Kunigund, which Elizabeth and which Agnes. Artists

[1] *Œuvres*, Vol. V, pp. 174, 186.

can be excused for doing this owing to the absence of real contemporary likenesses, but it is intolerable if people who write about the saints blot out all individual characteristics, and this even when we have exact historical information. This sort of biography is no rarity even to-day.

St. Francis de Sales repudiates this sort of hagiography. He severely criticises silence about the faults of the saints for the sake of dwelling on the virtues. Such one-sidedness falsifies historical truth and denies the individual character of all human perfection as it is willed by God. "There is no harm done to the saints," he said, "if their faults are shown as well as their virtues. But great harm is done to everybody by those hagiographers who slur over the faults, be it for the purpose of honouring the saints . . . or through the fear that our reverence for their holiness may be diminished. It is not as they think. These writers commit a wrong against the saints and against the whole of posterity. All great saints who write the lives of other saints tell of their faults and imperfections openly and impartially." For instance, St. Jerome speaks of the faults of St. Paula, whom he loved so much, as openly as he speaks of her virtues, "because he knew that one would be as valuable as the other ".[1]

The value of frank information becomes obvious when Francis says : "In spite of some imperfections they did not cease to be great saints and were highly pleasing to God. That should show us that we should not despair if we find in ourselves some imperfection or inclination which militates against true virtue, but we should resolve not to persevere in these faults." "We must mourn," he says somewhere else, "because we possess human and not

[1] *Œuvres*, Vol. X, pp. 345 *sq.*

angelic natures. Our imperfections ought to offend us
. . . but we should not be frightened and let our courage
melt away. . . . Of course God does not love our imperfections and peccadilloes, but in spite of these He loves us
very much." God can be satisfied with the religious soul
" in spite of the weakness of the human spirit ". Worldly
writers can emphasise the good points of their heroes and
conceal their faults, but the evangelists had another view,
so had " our Mother the Church ", and so had " old
biographers who demanded an account of faults and
sins ".[1]

This piece of advice is worth taking to heart for all who,
through a misguided preference for advertisement and
façade or through having some inferiority complex,
believe that they must whitewash the historical characters
of our wonderful saints. Just as in art the original form
of the mediæval statue is finer than the cheap and sugary
plastering done by a later hand, so also the historical
reality of a saint's life is far more valuable than inferior
biographies, both in beauty and in the power of impressing
people. This last point ought not to be forgotten, and
biographies which make saints so unreal as to prevent
anyone from hoping to imitate them, obviously have no
influence on life and still less on modern people. People
either excuse themselves or stifle every thought of imitation
by making a deep division between the life of sanctity
and their own. People say : those were saints, and we
are ordinary people. The Holy Father Pius XI expressly
condemned the affirmation " that those who reached the
summit of Christian perfection . . . had not to endure
the same human weaknesses and the same perils as other
men ". He referred to St. Francis de Sales as the saint

[1] Œuvres, Vol. VI, p. 248 ; Vol. XIX, p. 172 ; Vol. XVII, p. 41.

who recognised this error particularly clearly and refuted it.[1]

It is important not to forget that Francis de Sales is one of our greatest saints, a *Doctor Ecclesiæ*, and the doctor whom the Holy Father has singled out as the special patron of Catholic writers. And Francis did not give this criticism in a confidential letter to a friend but in the pulpit in a public sermon. He wished therefore to be heard by everybody. He referred to certain faults of the saints as publicly as to their virtues. This shows us how important he considered the doctrine of the individual stamp of human perfection to be. God alone is absolute perfection and the saints are only a relative reflection of God, according to their power of reflecting Him.

The imitation of the saints must be governed by this knowledge. We all know that youthful zeal seizes indiscriminately on all that is great and beautiful. It is only with oncoming age and increasing experience that people begin to sift what they have acquired and then to reject what is alien to their spirit. We see in the history of Christian asceticism a parallel to what happens in the development of the individual soul. In the first spring of asceticism in Egyptian monachism of the Fourth Century there was a naïf enthusiasm for imitating others. St. Anthony met a holy old hermit. He built himself a hut near his cell and tried to follow his example. Then he heard of another more rigorous hermit and visited him immediately so as to learn from him. And he tried to put into practice all that he saw on these journeys. " One must learn ascetical practices from someone," he preached to his followers, " then imitate him and try to equal him."

[1] Encyclical, *Rerum omnium perturbationem.*

The quotation shows the state of mind. People were full of admiration for every new feat of unheard-of austerity and tried to do the same and even, if possible, to go one better.

It must be admitted that this process of imitation has a certain educational value. St. Augustine, for instance, was encouraged by the thought that " others were able to do it so why should not I ? " This spirit has served throughout the centuries as a useful goad against lazy ease and self-satisfaction. But at the same time it should be recognised that there is a danger in stretching these principles too far. Such exaggeration resulted in the degeneration into an unchristian record-hunting in the field of asceticism, causing envy and jealousy on the part of those who were unable to compete. The striving after the unattainable often weakened the striving after the attainable. The Fathers of the Desert saw these unfortunate abuses and warned people against them. Francis de Sales, too, criticised " vain and jealous emulation ", which he said was the " peculiar imperfection of women and girls ". " It must be impressed on them," he writes, " not to want to do what others do." Those who go to communion often ought not to despise those who go seldom, and the latter " should not let themselves be carried away by vain emulation ".[1]

But the attempt to imitate all the saints or to copy only one in every particular is especially dangerous in that it may lead to a contradiction of the individual ideal of perfection which God has set for each person. This danger became more obvious the more theoretical research progressed and the more man became conscious of his individuality. The question could not be neglected in the

Œuvres, Vol. XVII, pp. 222 *sq.*

age of Humanism and the clear answer comes from St. Francis de Sales.

Francis knew how valuable it was to have an example to imitate and therefore he strongly recommended reading the lives of the saints. " Thou seest here as in a mirror the form of Christian life." But he adds immediately : " Apply the example of their behaviour to thyself, according to thy vocation." The slavish imitation of any saint must be excluded not only because many lives of saints " are material rather for admiration than for imitation ", but also because what is right for a given person in given circumstances cannot be applied indiscriminately to other people in other circumstances. Francis gives several examples of this. A married woman, like the historical *Philothea*, of course cannot go into the desert. But are the biographies of the Fathers of the Desert therefore of no use to her ? This does not follow. If she meditates on St. Paul, the first hermit, the necessary desire for solitude will be enkindled in her and make her able to withdraw herself now and again from daily life. She cannot imitate the complete poverty of St. Francis of Assisi. But she can and should imitate his love of poverty with certain " practices of real povery in the midst of riches ". The main benefit for her will lie in the applying to her own soul all that is most valuable and essential in the life of every saint, that is the unceasing colouring of her whole life with the holy love of God. " The saints were what we are . . . why should we not, following their example, do the same according to our condition and vocation ? " [1]

A young friend of St. Francis de Sales, Camus, the Bishop of Belley, describes an experience which throws some light on the views of our saint. Francis's fame as a

[1] *Œuvres*, Vol. III, p. 357.

preacher had decided Camus to imitate him in the pulpit. " I took pains," he confesses, " to adapt myself to his actions, his gestures, and his way of speaking." During a visit Francis turned the conversation round to this. " I have been told that it has taken your fancy to imitate the Bishop of Geneva in your sermons," he said. " Yes, indeed," I answered, " is he such a bad example ? " " O no, of course not," Francis replied, " he really does not preach so badly. But the worst of it is that you, as I hear, imitate him so badly. . . . By spoiling the Bishop of Belley you are not presenting the Bishop of Geneva. Joking apart, you are spoiling yourself. You are destroying a beautiful building so as to set up a new one against all the laws of nature and art. . . . If it were possible to exchange natural ability, what would I not give to be what you are ! "

Great examples are certainly very valuable, but though carefully studied they ought not to be copied. " I was no longer myself," admitted Camus. " I had spoilt my own original so as to make a very bad copy." He was led back to the right path by the clever advice of his great friend.

For perfection is not a ready-made form into which each individual can be moulded so as to become a ready-made saint. It is only the people whose field of vision is limited to their own ego who hold their system to be the only valuable one. They try with fanatical enthusiasm to force their model upon everybody. They are like the proverbial Procrustes who put his guests on his bed, cut off the legs that were too long, and stretched the short ones until they were long enough. The result was that people who were tortured in this way died, and if we apply this to the formation of personality the result is the same.

Francis de Sales struggled against any effort to make a personal ideal universally valid. Of course in so far as the soul is applied unceasingly to the will of God the perfection is the same ; but first of all we must find out what God wants of the individual according to his natural formation and according to the situation in the world to which He has called him.

(b) Personality

The task of all education and self-education is the formation, not the destruction, of character. From the point of view of natural ethics this is true because each man is formed differently. And the same can be said in moral theology, for grace does not destroy what nature gives, but crowns and fulfils it. Thus when Jean-Jacques Rousseau declared that the object of education was the unfolding of natural dispositions and not the crushing of them, he was saying what had been said a hundred years before in the same city of Annecy where Rousseau studied ; for it was there that St. Francis preached that the Catholic ideal of life was " to be completely what one is but in the best possible way ".

" Let us be completely what we are." This is the basic principle of the formation of character. Self-knowledge is therefore the first duty, and this involves not only the knowledge of our weaknesses and deficiencies but also the knowledge of our God-given virtues. Only by this knowledge of our personal uniqueness can we know rightly the lines along which we must develop and the goal for which God has created us. A mistaken knowledge of the real Ego obviously leads to a false idea of the goal to be attained. Deliberate self-deception would be a crime, a suicide, even if it were hidden under the cloak of humility. Accidental self-deception would be ethically blameless but none the less harmful for that. The danger of error lies where the subject and object of knowledge are confused, for it is obvious that we should judge the object from a standpoint of detachment and clarity. Self-judgment is a complicated matter. Each one of us knows more of himself than others know of him. What others know are the words and actions that are on the surface. Their motives, hidden to the outside eye, are knowable to our self-analysis alone.

Francis recommends an " open and frank " discussion with a spiritual director in addition to one's own judgment. The emphasis on this recommendation is not without its point, for it is a safeguard against the degeneration of the individual ideal of perfection as willed by God, into a foolish and capricious idol. Spiritual direction and the individual ideal are essential concomitants in St. Francis's system. By associating them the saint escapes two great dangers in the formation of character—first, the fitting of the character into a ready-made mould and, second, stupid conceit. Self-knowledge is the first essential, and recognition of the individual ideal the second. Their concurrence, it must be admitted, is often very difficult, for the farther the newly-discovered and right ideal is from the previous one, and the deeper the previous one is rooted in the soul, the more difficult the new one becomes. If the new ideal is higher, our desire for comfort opposes it because it requires that we should make greater efforts. We have already seen how the inclination to sloth tries to disguise itself behind humility. On the other hand, if the new ideal demands that we should aim lower and renounce the heights we had once dreamed of,

then our pride revolts, and our hurt vanity asserts itself
in phrases such as : " remaining true to oneself",
" being a hundred per cent. Catholic ", and so on.
Francis severely criticises both these efforts : he rejects
the " false and foolish humility " which buries the talent,
and equally the striving after an ideal which is too high.
" You can only give to God what you have." [1] Francis
had cogent ground for warning people against exaggeration. The mystical current, which came from Spain
at that time, overflowed France and Italy and brought
in its train a burning desire for the outstanding graces of
those specially endowed Spanish souls. Francis relates
that many people read books which promised to lead
them to the highest summits of mysticism. They dreamed,
he says, of " ecstasy and ravishment, of the union of the
soul with God, of a state where there was no more consciousness and feeling, but just elevation, transformation,
and perfection ". In their craving after the extraordinary
they yielded to " illusions, self-deception, and folly. . . .
While using the words and terminology peculiar to
mysticism, their natural spirituality and actual behaviour
remained on the bottom rung of the ladder. . . . They
believe they are angels but they are not even good men ".
" We must leave these super-terrestrial experiences to
super-endowed souls," says St. Francis, and behind his
words is the laughter of somebody who understands and
therefore forgives. " Our only purpose should be to
become devoted and religious men and women. . . . If
then it pleases God to raise us to perfection like the angels,
we will become good angels. But meanwhile we should
reconcile ourselves simply to being straightforward,
humble, and devout in the small virtues." Francis dis-

[1] *Œuvres*, Vol. XIV, p. 35.

courages people from reading edifying books which " are very sombre and come to us from across the mountains ". He prefers to recommend Scupoli's *Spiritual Struggle* which is " thoroughly clear, and practically arranged ". Even a soul so endowed with grace as that of St. Jane-Frances de Chantal he kept for years " in the lower planes " of asceticism before he opened the door to a higher mysticism. The restraint, lingering, and delay which precedes his taking people away from the ordinary way of life is a consequence of his experience. But Francis's rejection of any longing for an ideal which is not in accordance with the ability is not due to his experience of life, nor to any fear of the future and the possibility of risk—indeed, we will soon show that he is prepared to take more risks than most spiritual directors. No, his real reason is because of the will of God Who created the soul in a particular way and in no other. He wrote to Madame de Brulart, who was always striving beyond her capacity : " What would be the use of being the most marvellous creature of heaven if it were not according to God's will ? " " People laugh at a painter who wants to paint a horse but succeeds in painting a bull, however excellent. Be the work so beautiful in itself, it does little honour to a master who intends to produce something else. . . . We want to be what God wants us to be . . . and we do not want to be what we might easily be, but against His intention." [1]

True love of God leads human desire to conformity with the will of God. Therefore the perfect Christian joyfully affirms his personality as it was created by God. The refusal to do this is a sin from the religious point of view. But judged psychologically it is a characteristic expression

[1] *Œuvres*, Vol. XIII, p. 54.

of neuroticism. It has been referred to in the *Individual Psychology* of A. Adler. Both from natural and supernatural standpoints, we should crush any wish to be something other than what we really are, for such a wish is a transgression against the true ideal of holiness and destroys spiritual health. Here again we get an example of how religion and true humanity go hand in hand. The holy man is also the healthy man and the complete Christian is the complete personality.

Egotism can always find loopholes in this and neurotics can affirm, in their subtlety, that of course they want to be what God wills. And therefore they might say that because they wish to achieve the greatest things in His honour, they pray Him to improve their spiritual capacity. But even the longing " for greater understanding " or for " the means of serving God which we do not naturally possess " is to be condemned. St. Francis, usually so very mild, pulls to pieces such a wish in the heart of his " most beloved daughter ", St. Jane-Frances de Chantal, with irony. She certainly could not be called a neurotic type, but, as Rudolph Allers, a pupil of Adler, once remarked, " every man fundamentally speaking is capable of neurosis ". Even St. Francis is not free from it, though he overcomes it with his religious concentration. In a letter from St. Jane-Frances de Chantal, Francis noticed a sentence which, though apparently harmless, expressed a longing for perfection in a way that might lead in the neurotic direction. He recognised the danger immediately and removed it ruthlessly. " You say that you are much harmed by your weaknesses . . . that is most certainly a bad thing to say. How would you like your soul to be ? Clear-sighted, strong, decided and steadfast ?

Admit that your soul is measured according to your position—it is a widow's soul which is petty and subject to every degradation except insulting God." The blemishes " which God has left in us for His greater glory " do not at all hinder our realisation of our ideal self according to His will.[1]

Our development is influenced by the position we occupy in the world as well as by our natural abilities. This is not the place for talking about the religious importance of vocations, but it is certain that God wants there to be a variety of vocations and the form of perfection must be " different according to the vocation ". In a letter of 1604 Francis wrote : " People in religious orders, widows, and married people should all strive after perfection but not in the same way and in the same kind." Some years later he wrote in the *Introduction* : " I ask you, Philothea, would it be right if a bishop wanted to live a life as solitary as that of a Carthusian, if married people did not want to acquire more property than Capuchins, if a manual worker wanted to pass his whole day in Church like the religious orders, and if a religious always wanted to entangle himself in questions of law like a lawyer ? Would not such piety be comic, disordered, and improbable ? And yet one comes across this error very frequently." [2] No, " the practice of devotion must be different with the nobleman and the labourer, with the servant and the prince, the widow, the maiden and the married woman. It must . . . be measured according to the strength, occupation and duty of the individual ". A form of devotion which " harms the vocation " and " nullifies respect in the world, makes the spirit gloomy

---

[1] *Œuvres*, Vol. XIII, pp. 202, 282.
[2] *Œuvres*, Vol. XII, p. 268.

and the character intolerable " [1] is a false form of devotion.
And false are all the religious practices which cannot go
in harmony with one's God-given position in the world.
The saint advised the Duke of Bellgarde—a great man at
the frivolous court in Paris who had been converted to
religion—" to preserve spiritual standards carefully, in
palaces, galleries, and salons ; but "—what Francis added
is important—" let it be a wise, earnest, strong, inflexible,
yet pleasant and loveable spirituality ". According to
Francis, this prince was specially chosen to bear witness
at court to the " truth of heavenly love ", and this
personification of the truth of divine love—" *la verité,
l'amour céleste* "—was the appropriate retribution in case
the prince had sometimes defaulted through the vanity
of earthly love (" *Vanité des amours terrestres* ").[2] The
goal to be aimed at and the choice of the means should
be decided not from inclination but from duty, not from
personal opinion but the will of God. Francis lays
great emphasis on the importance of the person
subjectively, but he is far from allowing scope for
subjective caprice. The perfect Christian should try to
fulfil God's will and not his own, and in this way play his
part loyally in that condition of life to which God has
called him.

" Nothing," writes St. Francis to the countess, " hinders
our perfection in our actual condition so much as the
longing for another condition. For instead of working in
the field in which we are, we send our oxen and plough
into our neighbour's field in which we cannot reap. . . .
That is only a waste of time, for it is impossible for us to
turn our hearts to acquiring the virtues needed for our

[1] *Œuvres*, Vol. III, pp. 19 *sq.*
[2] *Œuvres*, Vol. XVI, pp. 195, 56 *sq.*

present condition when we let our thoughts and hopes roam about elsewhere." [1]

(c) Lay and Monastic Life

With a conviction of the correctness of the individual ideal of perfection Francis de Sales also criticises those manifestations of mystical enthusiasm which in his time made an extraordinary number of pious souls take flight from the world or long for the cloister. Married men wanted to leave their wives, their daughters, and their ageing parents, so as to enter into one of the flourishing convents. Some had the intention of starting a hermit life following the example of Ambroise Marian or Catharine of Cortona. And many, among them the widow Jane-Frances de Chantal, even conceived the adventurous plan of fleeing to the Holy Land so as to end their days there buried in God. The example of the Spaniards who emigrated to Mexico and imitated the harsh life of the Fathers of the Desert, found a following. It was held to be impossible to achieve perfection in the world. The exact following of the evangelical counsels was considered an almost essential step on the way to sanctity. " Only few souls save themselves in worldly life," wrote Francis's young contemporary, the Abbé of Saint-Cyran. This Abbé, his friend Jansenius, and the circle which collected round them, pushed this line of thought to an extreme after Francis's death. Francis combated this error with the truth that " it is as possible to reach highest perfection in the world as in the cloister ". " It would be an error, even a heresy, to try to ban religious life from the company of soldiers, the workrooms

[1] *Œuvres*, Vol. III, p. 261 ; Vol. XIII, pp. 206 *sq.*

of labourers, the court of princes, and the household of married people." [1] " The evangelical counsels were given not for the perfection of each individual but for the perfection of the Christian people as a whole." " God does not want each person to carry out all the counsels, but only those which suit him according to the circumstances of the time, the conditions of his life, and his strength. . . . If your parents really need your help, then it is not the time to go to a convent, because, in such circumstances, love commands you to fulfil the commandment ' honour, serve, support, and help thy father and thy mother '." It may be the duty of a prince to renounce virginity and obtain heirs in holy matrimony so as to defend his people from political unrest. In weak health one is forbidden by true love of God to adopt real poverty. Fathers of families cannot " sell all and give it to the poor " ; married people should not fly from one another. " In certain conditions and for certain individuals, the following of the counsels may be impossible, useless, dangerous and harmful." Our Lord says " he who can do it let him do it ".

There is one unique and universally valid principle : love of the divine will. It is through this love that one should go into the cloister or follow particular evangelical counsels, but the authority of this love will also advise many people to remain in the world to maintain their property, to marry, even to take hold of weapons and go off to war, " though this last may sometimes be very dangerous ".[2]

Francis has no desire to condemn the world in the severe terms of, for example, St. Athanasius's *Concerning*

---

[1] *Œuvres*, Vol. X, p. 59 ; Vol. III, pp. 320 *sq.*
[2] *Œuvres*, Vol. V, pp. 75 *sq.*

Virginity, a sort of condemnation which crops up repeatedly during the ages. Nor does he share with the Fathers of the Desert their burning enthusiasm for a life removed from the world. " Solitude, my paradise," cried St. Jerome. But we have often seen how the serpent forced its way into this paradise and for many the desert became a place of most difficult temptations. St. Teresa mentions this danger : " no clausura is too narrow . . . and no desert too vast for the devil not to come in ". " Solitude has its storm and the world its torments." Francis does not join in the extravagant songs of praise for the quiet cell removed from the world, and the renunciation of all human things, of the *Imitation of Christ*. He rejects still more strongly the " away from the world, back to solitude " of the Abbé de Saint-Cyran. Only the vocation God gives us can decide whether we ought to go into the desert with St. John the Baptist—since the Fourth Century he has always been a model of flight from the world—or whether we should live with Christ in the world, without being of the world. " Perfection does not consist in not seeing the world but in not giving oneself over to it inwardly." " If God's hand guides us, then all ways are good." Francis differs from many preachers who want to win all souls for the cloister. So as to make clear the gulf in the respective ideas, he has been compared with St. Jerome. Of course we must not forget that St. Jerome was confronted with the demoralisation of the Fourth Century. But however much we allow for the differences in time, a profound difference in the two conceptions still remains. St. Jerome is always forcing his friends to leave the world. St. Bernard followed in his footsteps with even greater emphasis. But Francis wanted his little twelve-year-old sister Joanna to leave a

convent after she had spent a year there, because "it is
unreasonable that a girl should be allowed to stay so long
in a convent, if she does not intend to spend her whole
life there". "What is wrong with somebody leaving
the novitiate if they find that they have no vocation to
religious life?" The saint asks this question and
answers: "Nothing, without a doubt." Francis admits
that of course one "cannot practise pure contemplative
devotion in the midst of the work of affairs in the world".
But besides this, there are "many other forms of devotion".
Each person ought to embrace the ideal he is called to
and he will achieve perfection.[1]

In his encyclical on the saint, Pius XI has made special
reference to this doctrine. "Francis de Sales appears
given to the Church through God's special decree so as
to counter that point of view deeply rooted in his time
and not yet overcome to-day which says that true saint-
liness . . . is so difficult to achieve that the majority of
the faithful could not possibly attain it . . . and also
that the urge to sanctity is bound up with such great toil
and difficulty that it is not generally achieved by men
and women outside the cloister." The Holy Father adds
that priests should therefore "encourage the faithful to
follow the sanctity corresponding to their state in life".

Deviation from the vocation which is God's will can
wreak a bitter revenge. "It has often happened," says
Francis, "that people who have preserved their holiness
in a world not particularly favourable to it, have lost it
in the solitude which appears so desirable for perfect
life."

Francis was careful to distinguish between the condition
of perfection which is grounded on religious vows and the

[1] *Œuvres*, Vol. XIII, p. 189 ; Vol. XV, p. 24 ; Vol. III, p. 21.

actual perfection which rests on the love of God. He is in complete agreement with the striking statements of St. Thomas Aquinas : " Many people bind themselves and do not keep their pledge ; others fulfil that to which they have not bound themselves. . . . Hence it can well happen that one person is perfect without being in the condition of perfection, and similarly that another lives in the condition of perfection without being perfect."

It is consistent on Francis's part, therefore, to refuse to accept the cloister-cum-secular life which until this time was considered to be the religious ideal for lay-folk. Devout people who were unable to carry out their heart's desire in a cloister, tried at least to imbue their lives in the world with the asceticism of the cloister. They chose poor clothes, wore penitential girdles, fasted severely, scourged themselves, scrupulously observed the prayer hours of the church, and took great pains to limit to the minimum their contact with men and earthly affairs. The edifying literature of the period subscribed to this ideal almost without exception and, according to Francis, preached " a form of religious life which leads to complete negation ".[1]

Some writings of St. Antoninus of Florence, who died in 1459, give us an instance of this view at the end of the Middle Ages. These writings are addressed to two holy women whom they advise to " withdraw from the world and live like a nun so far as this is in any way possible " ; " Flee from conversation with mankind ! " " Withdraw yourselves into solitude " ; " I condemn and forbid . . . " visits to theatres, weddings and other festivities. The soul should place a barricade between itself and contact with

[1] *Œuvres*, Vol. III, p. 6.

the world. Domestic duties should be left as much as possible to servants ; work that is to be done in the morning should be prepared the evening before so that the morning may remain free for prayer ; and if the soul is moved by religious thoughts during work then one should stop what one is doing and pray. He prescribes oral prayers that should occupy at least an hour every day, and in addition he recommends daily spiritual reading and the contemplation of the sufferings of Christ. There should, if possible, be the night offices and spiritual readings during meal-times. It is clear that Antoninus is at pains to fit the cloistered life into the life in the world. He nevertheless insists that the women addressed should fulfil their duties as married women and, when they protest, answers : " but I say to you that clothes do not make the monk but the good life ". This means simply that one can even live in the world as a nun.

Now both these holy women were in a position to realise most of Antoninus's advice. But in the following age this ideal was preached to the masses as a normal form of life. St. Teresa complains of " un-understanding directors " who told a married woman that " it was better if she prayed instead of looking after her household affairs even if it made her husband unhappy ". St. Teresa denounces such an attitude, saying that " such a director is unable to order either time or things ".

And now we see what happens if these ideas are carried too far. People thought " that no man could reach the height of Christian holiness if he lived in the pressure of temporal affairs ". And the result was, not that these people withdrew from the world, but that they abandoned the religious life altogether " as an impossible beginning ". Thus in the Fifteenth and Sixteenth Centuries religious life became utterly detached from the world, and secular life became irreligious.

St. Francis de Sales perceived the wrong of this, and affirmed that " the holiness of the cloister cannot be practised in a secular vocation ".[1] Fortunately Francis possessed not only the cardinal virtue of wisdom but also the great virtue of fortitude, and he interceded powerfully and yet with characteristic gentleness for the individual ideal of perfection which sanctifies every condition of life. In this way he hoped to cure the malady of the time. He himself pointed out the contradiction between his own and the usual conception in the *Introduction*. Religious literature in general advises a complete withdrawal from life, he says, but " my aim is to point out to those who live in towns, in families, and at Court . . . that a strong and resolute soul can live in the midst of the world without embracing worldly ideas, that sources of holiness can be found in the hardships of the world and that one can live among the flames of earthly desires without burning one's wings ". With the same peaceful decision which had helped him to struggle against the Calvinists as a youth, he now opposes the representatives of this " strange spirit of the age ". " I foresee that many people will say that it is only for those in religious orders to seek after holiness . . . but I, my dear reader, say that the attainment of perfection should lie pre-eminently with the Bishops because they take the highest place amongst men like the seraphim amongst angels." A glance at Francis's collected works shows that such a mention of his own dignity is very rare ; very rarely does he say : but I . . . *mais moy* . . . *je te dis*. This notable exception shows the great importance that Francis sets

[1] *Œuvres*, Vol. III p. 21.

by the individual ideal of perfection. It shows his determination to put an end to false conceptions and to define the right relationship between secular life and sanctity. The necessity of this synthesis had long been recognised, as all the religious literature of the Sixteenth Century testifies. Francis's contemporary, the great Cardinal Pierre de Bérulle, had attempted the work, but his leaning towards Augustinian pessimism caused the humanistic world to misunderstand him. Such a task had to be undertaken by a religious genius, by a man who united in himself holiness and knowledge of the world, and St. Francis was this " gentleman saint ". " Every precious stone shines in glowing light," he announced to the world, " but with its own particular lustre." [1]

(d) The " Individual Idea of Perfection " To-day

The humanists elevated the individual value of individual men to the greatest possible heights. This was not a new idea, but the previous centuries having undervalued it, it appeared as something new and was partly the cause of a new epoch in history. Individualism is one of the characteristic and fundamental currents which separates modern times from the Middle Ages. St. Francis sifted the valuable elements from this way of thinking and applied them to the Catholic formation of personality, proving that they were essential ingredients of the Christian ideal of perfection. But the secular philosophy which had split the Church in the last century exaggerated the right of the individual to despise his fellow-creature, and thus any sense of equality and co-operation was

[1] Œuvres, Vol. III, pp. 6, 9, 20.

crushed—a state of affairs that culminated in Nietzsche. The principle, however, was not logically tenable, and the fact that it murdered corporative society was soon observed. In this lay the positive value of Nietzsche's work. Catholic leaders were the first to raise their voices against this evil, and now everyone sees the real danger of the belief in a superman. St. Francis de Sales saw it long ago when he wrote about the rights and duties of individual holiness.

" Let us be completely what we are." Well, what are we ? We are accustomed to fill up forms which ask us our occupation, family condition, religion, etc. God Himself will one day ask us these questions and we will not satisfy Him if we ignore the God-willed ideal of the Catholic man—be it official, shop-keeper, labourer, husband, father, virgin—in favour of some self-created ideal. The position which God allots us in human society, in the Church, and in the State, binds us by obligation.

To be whole means to bring the whole strength of one's life to development. Jesus tells a parable of three servants, one of whom had to look after five talents, another two, and the last one. Two of the servants doubled the goods entrusted to them and therefore obtained reward. The profit was estimated according to the percentage of the capital lent and, rightly inter-preted, it was not the material success but the personal achievement which was valued. He who has received more has the greater obligation. What is the use then of comparing ourselves with others ? Such comparisons always end by our being convinced of our superiority : I am as religious as so-and-so, I do as much as so-and-so. This weighing of greater or less is worthless and ignominious because we can only judge of the result by the amount of strength we have to realise it with. " Give an account of your stewardship " the Lord Who gave us the talent will say. " Throw the useless servant into the exterior darkness " is the word of judgment against him who buries his talent instead of turning it to account.

This obligation to an individual ideal of perfection demands the right and free way of obtaining it. St. Francis de Sales preaches this throughout his life. According to him the way for millions is to stay in the world, to face the streets. If we want to do this, well and good ; if we prefer another system, equally well and good. Whether we proceed according to Salesian or Ignatian methods, whether we want to belong to the Benedictine or Franciscan community, we decide by our own free choice. But the decision which we make should not be the result of whim or caprice, but should be prompted by the continuous expression of our personality which discovers the good in the soul. Let us look at the two fundamental forms of religious life which we have already mentioned : the holiness deriving from the fear of God, and the holiness deriving from the love of God. A melancholy temperament, a converted sinner, would hardly incline to joy ; a joyous nature, a straightforward character, will not incline to fear. We have already referred to the various forces which unite to form a personality—heredity, environment, education, and the chances of fate. These are given by God. Let us not forget the direction of each individual soul through the grace of the Holy Ghost. We must always realise that the multiplicity of Catholic systems of life and the diversity of their conceptions are willed by God. The Church allows this variety. We have already seen how individual theologians and saints disagreed with one another and the Church raised no objection. She affirms freedom of opinion in the interest of individuality. She places limitations only where truth ceases and false-hood begins, where there is no longer the unfolding of life but the stifling of life.

Thus it is not the Church which cramps the individual ideal of perfection, but the individual souls themselves. Francis himself once said : " If we are enthusiastic about a certain practice we despise people who are not equally enthusiastic and carp at those who have different opinions from our own." Luis de Granada has expressed this even more clearly : " Good people often fall into the following error—as soon as they discover that they have made any progress in sanctity they are immediately convinced that there are no other means to this end save the ones they have chosen . . . they desire that everybody should make use of the same ones, warning all delinquents that they will not achieve eternal life . . . hence arise wicked judgments on others which cause disunity and dissension between people who should be brothers." [1] To-day we can make the same observation : in one's enthusiasm for one's own outlook on life one is inclined to scorn those who have a different outlook. History shows that even famous and holy people severely fought all opinions which were in contradiction to their own. In this they were wrong, although in other ways they were great. St. Francis de Sales affirms the right to individu-ality. " There is no point," he declares, " in setting me up as an example to other bishops. I am perfectly certain that they can justify their position in their own way, just as I can in mine." Francis is convinced of the rightness

[1] *Œuvres*, Vol. III, p. 258.

of his system, but he also recognised that other views may be good and useful even if he himself does not share them. " This method is good, but it is not mine," he once wrote. " If I am more interested in one thing than another, I hope by God's grace that I shall never be so obstinate and narrow as to condemn those who do not share my opinion. No, I certainly do not believe that my opinion must be the rule for the whole world . . . let each proceed according to his light so long as it be for the greater glory of God." [1]

The motto *in certis unitas, in dubiis libertas, in omnibus caritas*—Unity in certain things, liberty in doubtful things, charity in all things—expresses the spirit of St. Francis de Sales. " Let each proceed in his own way with the gifts he has received from God, but let each proceed with the same end in view—serving God." [2] In preaching his " *sanctitatis uniuscuiusque propriæ colendæ officium* ", the Holy Father Pius XI specially recommends St. Francis de Sales as the saint of our time. [3]

---

[1] *Œuvres*, Vol. XVII, p. 33 ; Vol. XII, p. 148 ; Vol. XVII, pp. 114 *sq.*
[2] *Œuvres*, Vol. XVII, pp. 222 *sq.*
[3] Encyclical *Rerum omnium perturbationem.*

PART THREE

LOVE OF GOD AS CENTRE OF LIFE

(i) LOVE AND PERFECTION

(a) Love of God

FROM youth onwards we are accustomed to look on love as the essence of perfection and to consider it as the goal of ethical effort. This is quite right. Man is created by God for God, and the extent to which his inner nature is bound with God conditions the degree of his perfection. Theologically considered, grace supports the bond with God ; psychologically considered, love does. The Bible defines the bond between man and God as a unity of love. " If anyone loves Me," says Christ, " my Father will love him, and we will come and make our dwelling with him." " Who remains in love dwells in God and God in him," declares St. John, and the apostle of the Gentiles preaches : " He who adheres to the Lord is one spirit with Him."

A glance at life may give us a clearer understanding of the idea " unity in love ", for it will show that in all things love brings men nearer to one another. As we saw, love involves some degree of similarity in the thoughts and outlook of those who love, and the ideas that they have in common increase continuously if imperceptibly. Thus love eliminates the narrow circle of egocentric self-consciousness and allows the beloved to be " half one's own self ". The *I* and the *thou* are moulded into the *we*.

The *thou* becomes another *I*, perhaps a better *I*. Beethoven and Wagner bear witness to this feeling of identification. Beethoven begins his letter to the " immortal beloved " : " My angel, my all, my ego," and concludes " always thine, always mine, always ours." Richard Wagner, in the duet in Act II of *Tristan and Isolde*, writes : " Thou Isolde, I Tristan, no more Tristan and Isolde . . . but one consciousness, boundless, eternal." The same phenomenon which we observe in the profane love of two classical musicians shines forth in the pure spiritual love of St. Francis de Sales and Jane-Frances de Chantal. The saint once wrote : " We want to obey God, you as I and I as you."

With Aristotle, Plato, and the Stoics, we find definitions of love and friendship as being the power which unifies and makes one. The theologians took over these definitions and affirmed that the psychological laws between man and man also ruled the relationship between man and God. The Fathers of the Church praise love as the bond of union between man and God. St. Thomas Aquinas recognises the essence of the love of God in the friendship between man and God by asserting that through love the beloved lives in the lover, just as, in the intellectual field, the known exists in the understanding as a psychical reality. The Christian mystics have strived to describe the experience of union with God, and they frequently, especially in the *Song of Songs*, compare it with marriage, hoping that the comparison with the most intimate love known to man here below may help the reader to understand the nature of unity with God.

Patristic, scholastic, speculative, and mystical theology consider love as the essential means to union with God.

All agree with St. Paul that "love is the bond of perfection". "Love," declared St. Francis de Sales, "is the universal means of salvation. . . . There is no salvation without love . . . hence our sweet Saviour ceaselessly longs for our love by which we are eternally saved." Christ knows that the contemplation of God's majesty, and its contrast with our misery, fills us with a feeling of such disparity that we might be discouraged from loving ; thus He declares that his attachment to us is full of love and commands us to love Him with our whole strength. " Perfection of life is perfection of love, for love is the life of our soul." [1]

One might perhaps ask why we observe the Commandments. The fact that we observe them is an obvious consequence of love, since he who loves does what the beloved wants. To separate love from obedience is to mistake the very essence of love. True love of God has to result in obedience to His Commandments and the practice of every other virtue. Thus Christ adds to the chief commandment of love : " in this commandment lies the whole law and the prophets ". According to the expressed declaration of Jesus, the observance of the whole law stands or falls by the fulfilment or the disregard of the chief commandment. St. John therefore reflects the doctrine of Jesus when he says : " that is the love of God, that we keep His commandments " ; and St. Paul declares : " The fulfilment of the law is love " ; while James describes love as " the royal law " which comprehends all ethics in itself ; for where love rules there God's will is fulfilled without ceasing.

St. Augustine, declaring that : " Holy scripture commands nothing but love ", strove to lead the Greek

[1] *Œuvres*, Vol. IV, p *iii sq.*

schema of the four cardinal virtues and all the ethical virtues back to love. He therefore considered that the fulfilment of all individual commandments is a consequence of love. Hence he affirms what seems to be such a daring phrase : " Love and do what you will." These expositions of St. Augustine have remained the standard for the moral theology of the Church. Scholasticism took them over as the foundation of its scientific work. Love, declared St. Thomas Aquinas, is the first or " the form " of all virtues. St. Francis de Sales quotes at the beginning of the *Traitté* the phrase : " the whole doctrine which the Church preaches is based on love ". " Love," he says later, " is the bond of perfection, because in it and through it all the perfections of the soul are united. Without it one could possess neither a modicum of all the virtues nor the perfection of any one single virtue." " The love of God is the goal, the completion, the crown of the Universe." Thus the greatest and first commandment gives all holy laws, all divine regulations, all sacred writings, their place and their dignity. Everything was made for this heavenly love—all counsels, admonishments, suggestions—and all the usual commandments hang " like leaves on the blessed tree of this commandment ".[1]

Unfortunately not all writers have sufficiently understood the central meaning of love. *The Shepherd* of Hermas, written in the Second Century, must be the first book in which love appears as a virtue amongst many others and equal to them. Other writings followed this. The whole group of the alphabetically arranged " *Summæ pro confessoribus* " of the late Middle Ages gives the same impression. Even more dangerous are the

[1] *Œuvres*, Vol. IV, p. 3.

attempts to place another virtue than love as superior to love. Thus Hermas describes Faith as the mother of all virtues, while Tertullian favours patience, Lactantius justice, and Ambrose piety. The acceptance of the ancient scheme of the four cardinal virtues, with justice and prudence at the top, had a wide influence on the systematisation of Christian doctrine and virtues. Besides justice there also appears, probably since the Fourth Century, the virtue of humility as the principal virtue. We have already referred to the significance of this doctrine in the ethical writings of the late Middle Ages. Of course these writers have not actually overlooked the importance of the chief commandment, but in so far as they place the first of all virtues on an equality with the others, or presented another as being more important, they obscured, perhaps unintentionally, the primacy of love and it is understandable that the readers of these writings looked on other virtues as the corner-stones of their religion. Love is the sun of all ethical life, from love every other virtue receives its worth from God, and the unity of love between the soul and God is the essence of perfection.

(b) The Way of Perfection

How then does one achieve this unity of love? The words of the Angel to Tobias seem to point the way : " Prayer with fasting and alms is better than heaping up treasures of gold." By prayer was understood the whole practice of honouring God, and in the Middle Ages this practice was divided into three parts : liturgical prayer ; fasting, self-conquest and mortification ; alms-giving and every kind of neighbourly love. These three were

considered necessary characteristics of a holy Christian.
The saints distinguished themselves in all these practices,
sometimes emphasising one and sometimes another,
depending on the epoch in which they lived. This trio
they saw as indispensable to perfection, but the question
was whether it was the cause of perfection or merely the
first step on the way.

If the trio was the cause then it should be able to
produce the consequence of itself. But that appears
questionable, because a social efficiency and a strict way
of life are possible without any relationship to God, as
history shows. History has shown us heroes of self-
mortification and men of social action quite outside the
theocentric circle of ideas. Moreover, liturgical prayer
will not produce inner sanctification simply through
correct repetition, but rather when an answering disposition animates the man who prays. Beyond mere
prayer, valuable in itself as it is, there must be a higher,
an inner relationship between the self and God, which
governs our individual acts.

What shall we call this ? Theology calls it love. But
could it not be expressed in a more dynamic way ? The
wish, and the effort to fulfil the wish, have been very
lively since the beginning of the new age. Humanism
had turned the eye of Fifteenth and Sixteenth Centuries
on to the fulness of life. The expression *ad fontes* (back
to the sources) inclined theology to exegetical studies of
Holy Scripture and to zealous reading of the original
works of the Fathers of the Church, rather than to the
collection of individual maxims so popular in the Middle
Ages. This desire to go back to the sources sent doctors
from their books back to sick-beds, and caused psycho-
logists to acquire their knowledge not only from the folios

of old masters but also from the observation of men. Scientific work, too, received a new impetus in a new direction. Moreover, age-old doctrines of speculative theology reappeared in fresh colours, as if lifted out of the difficult processes of thought and placed in such close contact with life that they were easily understandable.

And now, how about the path to the love of God ? Let us look at life. In what way do two men arrive at the unity of love ? By becoming fond of each other. How then can unity of love with God be attained ? God's love for man and His advances to meet man, *i.e.*, His bestowal of sanctifying grace and the three theological virtues are dogmatically established. The problem lies in the advances on man's side. This development should be ruled by the same psychical laws as the relationship between man and man, because we only have one soul. Love of God is the means of being bound up with God, and also, loving leads to the unity of love. Thus love is not only the essence of, but also the way to, perfection. St. Thomas has said that every *habitus* grows with practice. " Through the act of love, love grows." Luis de Granada says in addition : " Just as one becomes a good painter through painting . . . so through loving one becomes a great lover."

To have pointed out this truth quite clearly is one of the imperishable merits of the great master of religion and Humanism, St. Francis de Sales. The humanists and the religious writers of the preceding century had, especially in Italy, prepared the way,[1] and Francis was fully aware that he was reiterating an old doctrine, but putting it in a new light. " We seem to think," he once said to his nuns, " that perfection is a talent which one can possess

[1] F. Vincent, *François de Sales, directeur d'âmes* (Paris, 1927), pp. 154 *sq.*

straightaway and without any trouble if one can only discover the secret. But we are wrong, for there is no greater truth than this : that if we aspire after union with the Beloved, we need to have faith and to work in the love of God ; that is all." Francis has described in a letter how love is not one way, but the only way, to reach God and eternal life : " Feed my lambs, feed my sheep," said Christ to Peter. " But with what," asks the saint, " must one feed these sheep ? " With love itself ! For either they live by love, or they live not at all. There is no half-way between love and death. One must either die or love, because, as St. John says, " Who does not love remains in death ".

It is this love of God, too, which must inspire the famous trio of prayer, fasting, and alms-giving, if these three are going to lead to union with God. Paul declared that neither a faith which moves mountains, nor the giving of all possessions to the poor, nor chastisement of the body to annihilation, have any value if there is no love. The Fathers of the Church, and especially Augustine, have asserted that love is the foundation of moral life. " If God is man's highest good," declares Augustine, " and if the good life is the same as to strive for the highest good, then the good life is not other than to love God with one's whole heart, with one's whole soul, and with one's whole mind." He advances the strong opinion that " where love is lacking there can be no good word and no good action ". Scholasticism discussed this doctrine in detail and defended it against both lax and rigorist inter-pretations.

Admittedly six centuries elapsed between the world of Augustine and the world of Scholasticism, during which period of time the ideas concerning perfection were

maintained but no progress was made in their attainment. Why was this? The primitive peoples who had
overrun the ancient cultural world had first to accustom
themselves to this new culture—this period of development is called the early Middle Ages ; and these sons of
nature had more understanding for a material fact than
for the spiritual basis from which it derived. Augustine
had commanded that one should not judge the behaviour
of men from its exterior appearance but should look to
the hidden source. This penetrating gaze into the soul
was completely lacking in the primitive peoples. The
objective fact of a crime springs to the eye more readily
than the inner conflict and evil of its perpetrator.
Similarly a great achievement of charity or of self-
mortification is more admired than the holy will which
inspires it and which cannot be seen with the naked eye.
The visible and the tangible ruled the worldly law and
influenced ecclesiastical penitential discipline. If one
zealously studied and copied the writings of the Fathers,
one would be inevitably drawn into the spirit of the age
with its over-emphasis on external facts and its too small
regard for the will behind them.

The theologians of Scholasticism were well aware of
these weaknesses and fought them tirelessly. The extent
of their exertions can only be judged by someone who
has carefully studied their manuscripts. Of course it had
never been altogether forgotten that love gives their
inner value to all acts which should lead to perfection.
To take a comparison : if a shade is put over a bright
light, then the pictures on the shade spring to the eye
more clearly than the light itself. In the same way the
achievements of prayer, fasting, and alms-giving, and the
three vows of the Orders can often be seen more vividly

than the love of God which is what gives them light. Now, keeping to the simile of the light, St. Francis placed it before a picture. It is the same light and the same picture, but the position is new. Francis's achievement is to be valued not as a revolution but as an evolution, and this reveals itself here, as elsewhere, as a renaissance of Christian antiquity. The return to the original sources which was born of the spirit of Humanism, the deeper study of Holy Scripture and of the Fathers of the Church bore fruit in Francis's system.

The central part played by love in Francis's system becomes clear if we compare his conception of holiness with that of St. Thomas Aquinas. Thomas proceeds from the cardinal virtue of justice. Justice gives to each man what is his. It demands also that man should settle his account with regard to God. That happens through honour and service to God. Holiness, *devotio*, is the inclination of the will to acts of service to God. The love of God is the source of holiness "in so far as one is inclined to love and serve a friend". Devotion has the same sense which we associate with the expression : a devoted, *i.e.*, a devoted and serviceable servant.

Francis de Sales on the other hand begins not with abstract principles, but with the observation of life. What do the people of our time consider holiness to be ? "Whoever fasts considers himself very holy, even if his heart is full of hate . . . another considers himself holy if he repeats an innumerable amount of daily prayers, even if his lips forthwith pronounce sharp and insulting words against his neighbour. A third readily gives alms to the poor, but he is not ready to condescend to forgive his enemy. . . . All these people are usually considered holy, but they are so in no sense." Each of them " designs for himself a form of goodness according to his own whim and fancy, and it is therefore nothing but a phantom of holiness ". True and living holiness presumes the love of God ; in fact it is nothing but the true love of God. It should increase to such perfection that it drives us on not merely to do the good, but " to realise it perpetually and with a ready will ". Thus holiness is the highest form of active love which is not content merely to observe all the commandments of God but wishes to go forward to do as much good as is conceivably possible. Love and holiness are related to one another like fire and flame. "If love is spiritual fire then the blazing flame is holiness." [1]

What a vast broadening has been effected by this conception of holiness ! Thomas, too, proceeds from the source *devovere*—to consecrate or surrender oneself. But in the real mediæval outlook his thoughts were crystallised around that surrender to God which finds its expression in the *cultus*. Ephraim the Syrian had already said to his monks : " prayer should be preferred . . . and treasured more than the observance of all other precepts ". The rule of Macarius of Alexandria contains the same idea, and the West took it over from the East. " Nothing should be preferred to the divine service ! *operi dei nihil preponatur*," exhorts St. Benedict, the organiser of Western monasticism, in the 43rd chapter of his Rule. The liturgy was the pivot of Benedictine monastic life, and this attitude ruled the piety of the Middle Ages. St. Francis de Sales on the other hand never considers any one devotion to God as the only one. None of the three great types, prayer, fasting, and alms-giving, are sufficient of

[1] *Œuvres*, Vol. III, pp. 14–16.

themselves, and even all three together do not fulfil the full conception of holiness. This full conception requires an enduring preparedness for, and practice of, the concentration of the whole strength on the realisation of the divine will. Holiness, love, perfection—these three words mean almost the same thing in Francis's conception.

With Thomas love stands in the background as the source and cause of holiness. In the foreground is the Lord of heaven and earth to Whom man owes devotion and homage. With Francis this picture of lord and servant is completely cut out in favour of the idea of the loving father who awaits his child. Love is the central point, but holiness is identical with love and demands the highest form of active love. Through it the soul mounts upwards " in high flight " to God. It wishes to be and to behave as is pleasing to God. But what is pleasing to God ? That which the development of ourselves demands. God loves us and desires that we should love Him in return, but "not because it lies in His interests, but in ours. For Him our love is useless, but for us it is very useful. And for that reason it is very pleasant to us ". The idea that God created the world not from any obligation but from the desire to share had already been announced by St. Thomas. Francis leads these ideas to completion and makes them helpful for Catholic holiness. We have already seen that man is created by God for God. God made man to love Him and put the predisposition for this love in man's soul. If man follows his inclination, it leads to the glory of God and to the highest development of man. So, in the Salesian system, the *utile à vostre âme* (useful for your soul) is placed second to the *agréable à Dieu*, because it is a result of the love of God and an almost equally important motive of the ethical struggle.

(c) Psychology of Love

According to the doctrine of St. Francis de Sales, then, love—in the sense of unity of love—is the essence of perfection ; and love—in the sense of the striving of love—is the way to perfection. The same word describes the goal and the means to the goal, but in a different sense. This change in the sense of the word as well as the point of using the word in both contexts will become clear as soon as we analyse psychologically the phenomenon of love. In the *Traitté*, which, by Francis's intention, provides the " history of love " on a scientific basis, the saint describes the psychical evolution of love. The origins of love are the complementary qualities of subject and object which we discussed earlier. The knowledge of this *correspondence* awakens the feeling of fondness, and this arouses the effort of the will which forthwith accomplishes the acts which attain the good desired, and pursues other efforts until the goal which is the union with the beloved is reached. These five stages constitute the essence of love, and thus love is comparable to a tree whose root is the projecting of the knowledge on to the good ; the base of the tree is fondness, and the trunk is the progress of the will ; the other efforts are the branches, and the joy in union is comparable to the fruit.

The idea of this comparison came to Francis from Spain. Luis of Granada had written : " Love is like the tree of life in Paradise ". And he carried this comparison through in four different illustrations : " The root is the first taste . . . of the beauty of the love of God . . . the

trunk is the glowing longing after so valuable a good.
. . . The branches are the virtues and the efforts pro-
duced by the longing, . . . and finally the fruit is union
with God ". Ludovicus Vivès, the leader of the Spanish
humanists, had expounded the nature of love in a five-
fold division and altogether shows such a great similarity
with Francis's idea that we are forced to conclude that
the saint knew Vivès' work. Besides this, it is certain
that Francis knew the *Summa* of St. Thomas Aquinas, as
an observation in the manuscript, omitted in publication,
shows.

But Francis was not a man simply to take over the
thoughts of his predecessors. He examined every doctrine
critically and sifted the knowledge which he had acquired
by self-analysis and the observation of his surroundings.
He thus arrived at his own opinion which he expounded
deliberately in the face of traditional opinion. We
noticed the independence of his thought when he defined
the foundation of love as being complementary qualities
and not merely of similar qualities, and this independence
of judgment is equally evident in the question of the
essence of love. Thomas saw it as fondness ; Ludovicus
Vivès in " firm friendship ". Francis declares : " the
unique nature of love consists in the movement and rush
of the heart which follows fondness and culminates in
union ". " Certainly love can be no other than movement towards the good." Fondness is described as the
support and carrier of this movement of the will and is
therefore an inseparable accompaniment of love, but it is
not the essence of love.

If we apply this analysis to the love of God, we find
that the unity of love with God is the essence of perfection. But the degree of perfection depends upon the

inner quality of this union, and as an unbroken concentration of all our forces on God is impossible here
below, so absolute perfection is reserved for the next
world. The perfection of this world is always relative.
Even with the saints it is only the *best possible* union with
God.

(d) Love and Justice

Let us again look back to the Middle Ages. At that
time it was Justice that ruled spiritual life, and this had
its influence on the mediæval form of devotion. " God is
love " was, of course, affirmed, but " God is justice " was
particularly emphasised. Augustine wrote : " The
greatest reason for the incarnation of Christ is the will of
God to show us His love ". But in another place he
expresses the opinion that without the fall the Word would
not have become flesh. The scholastics with Anselm of
Canterbury at their head solved the question from the
point of view of justice : to the injured majesty of God
there must be offered a fully valued sacrifice. Only the
death of Christ could provide full satisfaction for the
divine penal jurisdiction. Not without reason has a
" juridical theory of satisfaction " been spoken of. Moreover, certain theories about the sacrifice of the mass and
the expression " immolation of Christ " reflect these
thoughts later on. J. Pohle said : " In any case the pure
juridical theory of satisfaction must be completed and
deepened by the ethical theory of reconciliation ".
If we look at the moral theology of that time we find
that the influence of juridical thought is very marked.
" Moral theology under the influence of law " will form
a very important chapter in a history of moral theology

which is yet to be written. And what of religious life itself, with its material way of estimating achievements and its fear before the terrible judge? A glance at the art of the time shows us the spirit of the age. Think of the crucifixion at the altar of Grunewald! That is the sacrifice offered to divine justice for the sins of man. In Christian antiquity such a presentation would have been impossible, for people prayed in front of pictures of the Good Shepherd. Then there is the dance of death and the hymn for the dead, the *Dies Iræ* : " day of anger . . . what cries when the judge comes who will examine all things ! . . . nothing is unavenged . . . king of majesty before whom I tremble . . . deliver me, source of goodness, just judge, vouchsafe the grace of pardon before the day of reckoning ".

It would, of course, be a mistake to ascribe this emphasis on justice exclusively to the Middle Ages, just as it would be misleading to ascribe to St. Francis de Sales alone the emphasis on love. " God is Justice " and " God is Love ". Both truths have been affirmed at all times by Christian thought. But the relationship between the two has not always remained the same. In the Middle Ages they confronted one another and thought centred round one or the other. Consequently the two lines of thought were repeatedly in conflict, and it is here that the essential merit of Francis de Sales lies. He placed himself entirely in the spirit of Jesus with love at the summit. He declared it was the one principle running through all religion. " Everything in the Church belongs to love, happens in love, for love, and from love." [1] Love is not only the essence of, but it is also the way to, perfection. On this doctrine is based the unity of the Salesian system, and in this doctrine lies the valuable progress over and beyond St. Ignatius of Loyola.

It has been said " that in the Exercises Ignatius does not show love as the goal of, and way to, Christian holiness ". The Ignatian system emphasises the " most Holy Majesty " of God ; God, " the Creator and Lord " ; Christ " our Lord the Eternal King "—man owes to Him by right an unlimited sacrifice. Therefore St. Ignatius puts at the summit of his Exercises and as a major thesis the well-known declaration about the aim of human existence : " Man is created so that he may praise God his Lord, may respect Him and serve Him so as to achieve salvation." The legal relationship and the idea of King conditions his religious thought. Doubtless love will awaken later, but St. Francis de Sales from the first moment considers love to be the central point. In his words, the first sentence of the Exercises would have been : Man is created by God so as to love Him and thus achieve holiness.

(ii) THE DIVINE WILL

(a) *The Divine Will*

St. Thomas Aquinas has said : Man, like every other being, carries within himself by virtue of his nature and creation the germ of his completion and also his longing for it. Man, however, is created after God's image, and thus the development of his personality realises itself necessarily in the development of his likeness to God. Thus the goal of our life is the conformity of our thought and will with the divine intellect and will. This is the condition of the blessed in Heaven, and as this world is a preparation for the next our life work should consist in comprehending the divine truths and conforming our wishes with the Divine Will.

The same is demanded by St. Ignatius in his Exercises. It is man's duty " to offer his will and his liberty to God, so that the Divine Majesty may dispose of them according to His most holy will ". " Take and accept, O Lord," prays Ignatius, " all my liberty, my memory, my under-standing and my whole will, all that I have and possess. Thou gavest it to me, O Lord, and I return it. All is Thine, dispose of it according to Thy will." St. Teresa looks on the conformity of man's will with the will of God as a direct consequence of love, and declares : " All perfection which can be attained on the path of spiritual life consists in fashioning one's will in conformity with the will of God." St. Francis de Sales follows the line of these truths. The more love comprehends the whole man the more it urges him to an unreserved sacrifice to God. " Do we not see," writes the saint, " that a maiden on the threshold of unselfish love freely desires to be subject to her husband ? . . . that a nobleman wishes to subject himself to the prince ? similarly if we through a holy and unselfish love place all our inclinations in the hands of Divine love, so that they may be fashioned to the will of God, then begins the conformity of our heart with the heart of God." Francis dedicates the whole of the eighth book of the *Traitté* to " this love of conformity through which we unite our will with the Divine will ". We see in his letters the way he applies his theory in the directing of souls. Again and again he emphasises : " Let God's will decide ", " Man must serve God as God wills ", " Man must go the way which God leads—it does not matter where the way leads humanly speaking, for all ways are good if God leads us by the hand ".[1]

What does Francis mean by God's will ? He sees the will of God not merely in the commandments, not merely in the counsels of the Gospel, and not merely in the inspirations of grace : he sees it in every detail of our life. The daily work, the difficulties and obstacles that stand in our way, the pain and misfortune which obstruct our efforts, the death of our love—all is either willed or permitted by God. Hence it is our duty to accept our lot in so far as it corresponds to God's will, and to have that attitude to God-allowed blows of fate which God expects from a believing soul.

We have all known from our youth the maxim that where there is no commandment there is no duty and therefore no sin. But this maxim narrows down the will of God to the limits of written commandments, and thus a wide field is left to one's own imagination and one's own conjectures. Francis turns against this narrowing-down of the conception of the love of God. An arid and indigent love which limits itself to the minimum commanded achieves that lowest measure of personal development which is necessary so as not to be rejected from God forever, and this will never lead to the highest Christian perfection. Giving to God on command, as it were, and only as much as the command compels, can in no way answer to the idea of true and deep love. " The resolution to do no wrong is not enough," declares Francis, " one must rather resolve to do the maximum amount of good." Like St. Bernard, Francis holds that " the sufficient is not enough in the field of the love of God ". His ideal is : " *le très désidérable amour de la généreuse perfection* "—that

[1] *Œuvres*, Vol. XIV, p. 13 ; Vol. XII, p. 387 ; Vol. XIII, pp. 4, 141.

noble, lofty and courageous love which knows no economy nor stint in lavishing itself.[1] " Cowardly and languid " are those souls who set limits to their love. Therefore besides God's will we must also satisfy God's pleasure. The unreserved giving of our hearts " to God's will and pleasure " is his goal.

(b) Surrender to God

Perfect surrender presupposed two things : that the whole will of God should be affirmed, and that the recognition of it should follow from the whole soul.

Perfection demands, first of all, positive loyalty—loyalty not only as regards the problems in our life where important decisions are to be made, important tasks to be accomplished, and grave misfortunes to be endured ; but also in the least most insignificant detail. Every average day, with its little demands and meaningless misfortunes, shows the necessity of this. St. Francis says : " Show your loving concurrence with God's will, not only when something extraordinary happens, but more particularly in the trivial daily round . . . and do so with a calm and joyous heart." " Important matters and great decisions do not always come our way, but hourly there are small decisions to make." Francis sees through the Quixotry of certain souls who dream of extraordinary situations in life and heroically overcome the greatest difficulties which their imagination conjures up. He recognises the danger of this self-deception and playing with thoughts. The heroic decision to take some heavy cross upon oneself, which the future could but probably will not bring, means very little in the world of reality.

[1] *Œuvres*, Vol. XIII, p. 248.

" Frequently people reach heroic heights of love in their imaginations . . . and in real life they flee from any opportunities of taking up lighter crosses." They affirm that they are ready to die for their friends, yet refuse to place themselves at the service of their friends. They would pledge their life, but not their purse. Hence Francis warns us against these *ardeurs imaginaires*. " God defend us from such conceited zeal." Francis wants to see acts, however small, performed with great love. He wants us to conform to the will of God in the thousand small difficulties which confront us every day, and he is convinced that this constancy in little things is the most effective way of preparing ourselves for the longed-for harmony of our will with the will of God in great things.[1]

Perfection is not only accepted by the will but affirmed by the whole soul and the whole heart, and the whole strength. Man is not pure will ; body and spirit are united in him, and on the frontier between these two lies the kingdom of sentiment and the strength of the emotional life. The whole man must go into the service of loving God and not the will alone, and thus the emotional faculties, too, should be put in the service of the Creator. The characteristic expression of perfect surrender is joy. Aristotle said that " joyful action is an essential part of virtue ". " He is not good who has no joy in good actions," and he who overcomes a difficult situation with disgust is not brave but cowardly. In ancient Christianity the same idea was preached in the so-called Epistle to Barnabas : " To love joyfully and to work cheerfully is the testimony of virtue ". Scholasticism had bound up Catholic moral theology with the Aristotelian doctrine

[1] *Œuvres*, Vol. XIV, p. 122 ; Vol. V, p. 329 ; Vol. V, pp. 196 *sq.*

of virtues. " The virtuous," declared Thomas, " realises
the good with joy," and this realisation corresponds to
the spiritual condition. Francis was of the same opinion.
The soul should assent to the will of God " with joy ".
We possess purity of heart only " when our whole will in
all things, even in the smallest things, is freely and joyfully
subject to the most holy will of God ". It is one of the
most important maxims on the way to perfection that
" man must consider what God wills, and when this is
ascertained he must try to realise it joyously or at least
courageously ". But Francis is not satisfied with this
alone ; he adds : " not only that—one must love this
will of God and likewise the obligation it imposes on us.
And if it should so happen that we must look after swine
all our lives and do the most despicable things we should
nevertheless love it. It should be all the same to us in
what place God has put us. This is the summit of perfection for which we must all strive, and he who approaches
nearest carries the prize ". St. Francis once wrote to
Madame de Chantal : " In such circumstances would
you not throw yourself down before God and say to
Him quite simply : ' Yes, Lord, if Thou will it I
will it too, and if Thou will it not, then neither do I
will it '." [1]

Francis demands complete surrender to God to the
very end. Thus if a man goes against the realisation of
his own will, and, instead of saying " I will " says " I
surely might ", he is doing wrong. No, the heart should
not permit itself to have any wish of its own ; it should
renounce its own tendencies entirely so as to see only
what is God's will. Francis's ideal goes considerably
beyond the usual exhortation to yield to God's will. He

[1] *Œuvres*, Vol. XIV, p. 122 ; Vol. XIII, pp. 39, 20 *sq.*, 374.

does not want yielding, but conformity. He contrasts the two thus : " Yielding prefers the will of God to all things, yet does not cease to love many other things besides the will of God. Conforming breeds an indifference to all earthly desires and stands higher than yielding, for it loves nothing unless it be by and through its love for the will of God." [1]

When union with God has reached this height, all individual wishes are silent. The soul " asks for nothing and refuses nothing, but leaves itself in the hands of Divine Providence ". [2] Francis explains this state by means of a parable. " The daughter of a prominent doctor fell sick with fever." The father proposed blood-letting, and the daughter answered : " ' Dear father, I am your child, and I know not why I should want to become healthy. You must do for me what seems good to you. For me it is enough that I love you.' And the father bound the arm, set the lancet on the vein, and made the prick. The beloved child looked neither at her arm nor at the flowing blood : she did not turn her eyes from the face of her father. She only said tenderly : ' My father loves me very much, and I am entirely his '."

The counterpart of perfect love is perfect trust, for love inspires that trustful surrender to God through which one's own wishes withdraw into darkness. " Love," says St. John Chrysostom, " finds similarity or else strives after it." " Through the strength of being agreeable to God one will conform to God. Our will re-forms itself in the will of the Divine Majesty." [3] There is a certain identity between the human and the divine will. In the year

---

[1] Œuvres, Vol. V, p. 119.
[2] Œuvres, Vol. VI, p. 384.
[3] Œuvres, Vol. V, p. 60.

1607 Francis describes a trial as "a testing of our dear
divine will", and adds "I say our *divine* will, because if
we only wish for what God wills then His will and our
will are one will". In the *Traitté* he goes further and
says : "The loving soul may conform to the will of God
in the measure in which it merits it . . . non-Christians
carry their wills in their hearts, but every true child of
Christ rejects his will. Only then can one Will inspire
all souls and all hearts, rule them and guide them—the
Will of God." "It will change them all so that the will
of all Christians, and the will of our Lord will become one
Will." [1]

St. Francis de Sales himself lived in this perfect union
with God. For instance, he once wrote quite simply
what was almost too obvious to say : "If it does not
please God, then it does not please me." [2] St. Jane-
Frances de Chantal testifies that "his heart was completely indifferent to all things unless they were for the
satisfaction of God".

(iii) HOLY INDIFFERENCE

What is the possibility of our attaining this desired
union with God ? St. Francis de Sales says that man is
by his very nature a "middle-being". Through his
intellectual ability he shares the nature of the angels and
through his senses the nature of the animals. Thus two
ways are open to him : he can ascend to the spiritual and
divine and become like the angels, or he can descend into
the world of the senses and become like the beasts. It is
the function of the will to determine the direction he will

---

[1] *Œuvres*, Vol. XIII, p. 339 ; Vol. V, p. 78.
[2] *Œuvres*, Vol. XIV, p. 71.

take. The will has freedom of choice and can establish the direction because it rules like a king over all the forces of the human microcosm. But whichever way a man may go he leaves behind him his initial half-way position between angel and beast. He experiences an ecstasy, *i.e.*, a *sortie* from the initial condition of a " middle-being ".

Francis upholds this theory of ecstasy by reference to the " old philosophers " who " knew that there were two kinds of ecstasy, one which lifts us above ourselves and the other which drags us below ourselves ".[1] Plato is the father of this doctrine. In the *Phædrus* he depicts the soul in the guise of a chariot-driver who has two steeds to his chariot. One of these presses upwards to Heaven, the other downwards to earth. " Two ruling and leading inclinations," continues Plato, " are in each of us : the lust of the sensual for pleasure and the urge of the intelligent to good. Hence we have two sorts of extravagance : one coming from human weakness and the other from divine rapture." This Platonic doctrine was taken over by Dionysius the Areopagite and Augustine, but it was discredited by the scholastics and St. Thomas. The Renaissance, however, brought Plato into the foreground again at the expense of Aristotle, and Marcilio Ficino, the founder of the Platonic Academy in Florence, placed the double ecstasy side by side with the double love. Through animal love and animal ecstasy " man sinks from the height of his nature and is nearly a beast " ; but that love and " enthusiasm . . . which God infuses into us raises man above his nature and metamorphoses him into God ". Francis de Sales must have known this doctrine of Marcilio Ficino. The old philosophers to

[1] *Œuvres*, Vol. IV, p. 57.

whom he refers are first Plato and then Dionysius the Areopagite.

The upward ecstasy, *i.e.*, the climbing to union with God, is the goal of religious effort. Francis prays enthusiastically for this happy " drunkenness ". The state common to ecstasy and drunkenness is the " being out of oneself ". " O spiritual drunkenness," cries Francis, " which, in contradistinction to physical drunkenness, robs not the spirit but the body of its senses ! It neither stupefies nor brutalises, but rather renders divine . . . so that we live more in God than in ourselves, and think only of contemplating His beauty with love and aspiring to unite ourselves with His goodness." [1]

Now, how does one attain this supernatural ecstasy ? Francis's psychological penetration had shown him that, in the kingdom of the spirit as in the physical world, the law holds that extent and intensity of achievement are in inverse proportion to each other.

The more the soul has to do, the less perfectly does it accomplish its work ; for the soul is a limited being and hence its energy is limited. If it devotes its energy to a variety of things it gives less to each one. " To love many things equally " means " to love each in a less strong and less perfect way, for our capacity for love is limited . . . hence we ought not to divide our love but concentrate it on one thing as much as possible." [2] Concentration is the means to success in profane as in religious life, because only through the union of all forces on one goal may we realise the highest capacity of achievement.

Now observation of life confirms the idea that every really deep love necessitates the placing of all our strength

[1] *Œuvres*, Vol. IV, p. 325.
[2] *Œuvres*, Vol. IV, pp. 55 *sq.*

in its service. Francis is clearly aware of this. " The will," he writes, " rules all the forces of the human spirit ; but it itself is ruled by love." This is especially true of the love of God. " To rule and command is so inseparably part of love's essence that it ceases to be . . . where it is not master." " *Ou roy ou rien* " (king or nothing) is its motto. " It cannot live without reigning, and it cannot reign save as a sovereign." [1] Then Francis shows how love assembles all spiritual and sensual forces in its service and crushes physical life under its omnipotence. The cause is that the soul is the bearer of spiritual, sensual, and physical life, and because of this unity of human life every violent movement of one sphere extends over the others.

This concentration is the natural consequence of highly developed love, and it is also the means that nature puts at our disposal to increase love to its highest intensity. To concentrate on one thing, however, means to turn one's attention away from other things ; it necessitates an indifference to other aims. " Powerful love," declares Francis, " drags the soul so violently to the beloved object and occupies it so entirely, that all sensual and intellectual activities are abandoned. Yes, it appears that the soul, so as to nourish and develop this love, carelessly abandons every other activity." Francis refers to Plato who depicted love as " poor and naked ", and also to the phrase in the *Song of Songs*, " stronger than death is love ", and he further remarks that " as death drags the soul from all things with a strong hand so love separates the soul from all other inclinations and purifies it from all admixture ".[2]

[1] *Œuvres*, Vol. IV, p. 38.
[2] *Œuvres*, Vol. IV, p. 356 ; Vol. V, p. 211.

Powerful love has therefore a positive effect—concentration of all forces on the beloved object, and a negative effect—indifference to all other things. But if the means to the highest unfolding of the love of God is concentration which involves the throwing off of dependence on other things, then there must be a great equanimity concerning all earthly things. The history of Christian asceticism testifies to this truth. The abstention from marriage, the renunciation of possessions, the retirement from the world are nothing else but the throwing off of earthly things so as to concentrate on the one love.

Logically, therefore, Francis puts the duty of indifference beside the necessity for concentration. He praises *sainte indifférence* tirelessly saying that it alone guarantees that " spirit of the beloved children of God " who, fearlessly and in any circumstances, " follow the known will of God ". " This holy indifference must penetrate every aspect of natural life, such as health, sickness, beauty, ugliness, strength and weakness, and all things to do with civic life, such as honour, rank and wealth, and all the different conditions of spiritual life, such as aridity and ecstasy, and finally all behaviour and all suffering and every event which may ever happen." [1] Let us compare this with the fundamental truth of the Exercises. St. Ignatius says : " It is necessary to despise ourselves . . . so that for ourselves we want health no more than sickness, riches no more than poverty, honour no more than disgrace, a long life no more than a short life, and so on in all things." The agreement of St. Francis de Sales, who had been a Jesuit pupil in Paris, with the doctrine of St. Ignatius is well known.

[1] *Œuvres,* Vol. XII, p. 363 ; Vol. V, p. 122.

Francis bases his own life and the life of the souls under his direction on this theory. His major maxim is : " A heart that wants to love God must be intent only on loving God." The question : " Does love always reign in your heart ? " is the religious counterpart of the daily question : " How are you ? " Both questions arise from an affectionate interest in the most important good things of life, and both manifest the desire that our lives should flourish in the religious and the earthly spheres. All actions in the spiritual life have one and the same object, which is the orientation of all love towards God and the freeing of the heart of every other attachment. This principle was enunciated before Francis by Brother Egidius, one of the first companions of St. Francis of Assisi. " The one to the One," he said, i.e., " Give thy whole soul, namely the one, to God alone, the One." [1]

We find this idea most beautifully and clearly expressed in Francis's letters to St. Jane-Frances de Chantal. " Our heart," he wrote in December 1605, " you see, I say *our* heart, is created from the holy love of God." " We belong entirely to God, without reserve, without division, without any exception, without any other striving. . . . If we had only the minutest fibre of love in our hearts which was not for Him and from Him, we would, O God, tear it out straight away." [2] Again and again he advises that we should " try to repeat this truth : my Beloved is mine and I am His. Examine and see if perhaps some force or other of your soul, or some sense of your body, does not belong to God . . . and should you discover such a thing then take it out . . . all of you must belong to Him ". " Life and death, all our relations, we should

[1] *Œuvres*, Vol. IV, p. 278.
[2] *Œuvres*, Vol. XIII, pp. 133, 200.

leave purely and simply to Divine Providence." [1] Of
course in sickness it is advisable to call for medical help,
but still, " one should await the result as peacefully as
possible with a decision to adapt oneself entirely to the
Divine Will ".[2] This " spirit of freedom and equanimity "
must also rule our work for God's honour. " For instance,
this Lent, I ought to preach in a little place in my diocese,
but if I am ill or break my leg, that is no reason to become
sad or upset . . . for it is quite certainly the will of God
that I should serve Him through suffering and not through
preaching." One should look on it as a fault if holy
people are depressed when duty calls them unexpectedly
from their usual round of devotions. Holy indifference
should exist with regard to unavoidable changes of mood
—changes from joy and inspiration to depression and
exhaustion, because " why should it worry us if we wander
through the deserts if only God is with us and we are
going to Paradise ? " [3] And Francis refers to Christ on
the Mount of Olives as a perpetual example of holy
resignation : " After Our Lord on the Mount of Olives
had prayed to His Father for consolation knowing that
He would not give it Him, He thought no more of it
but carried through the work of our redemption as
boldly and courageously as if He had never desired
consolation." [4]

In their mutual love Francis felt Madame de Chantal's
lack of consolation as his own pain. He made up a
prayer for her : " No, Lord, I want no more satisfaction
from my belief, my hope and my love. . . . Alas, Lord,
if it is pleasing to Thee that I should have no joy in the

[1] Œuvres, Vol. XIII, p. 182 ; Vol. XIV, p. 106.
[2] Œuvres, Vol. XV, p. 375.
[3] Œuvres, Vol. XII, pp. 364 sq. ; Vol. XIII, p. 5.
[4] Œuvres, Vol. XIII, p. 6.

practice of virtue . . . then I assent with the whole strength of my will, even if it is against the feelings of my will." The yearning for holy indifference increased with Francis after the year 1611, and became the most bold renunciation : " My beloved daughter, when will we finally be quite dead before God so as to live again in the new life in which we ourselves will have no wills . . . except to let God's living will rule our quite dead will." [1]

Francis's life provided (repeatedly) the proof of the genuineness of these words ; for example, there was his friendship with Madame de Chantal itself. From the very first moment, the only question which they asked was—what is God's will ? This holy friendship began through love of God and they were both prepared to experience separation at God's hand. When Madame de Chantal was nearing death in 1612, Francis wrote to a priest : " Her serious illness has led me to fasten my prayers on to the third petition of the Our Father : Thy Will be done ! I am quite submissive to the will of God. If it pleases Him to take this mother from us, His Holy name be praised ; if it pleases Him to leave her, His Holy name be praised ! " [2] Madame de Chantal proved herself his true pupil when in 1623 she received the news of his sudden death. First she broke down, but then her love for God flared up and she said : " I have no word to say but can only worship in deep silence the eternal wisdom of God Who has drawn me back from death so often in order that I should suffer this deepest pain of all —to see myself suddenly robbed of the only consolation which remained to me in this life."

[1] *Œuvres*, Vol. XV, pp. 161, 198.
[2] *Œuvres*, Vol. XV, p. 170.

But in the midst of her lamentation sounded the heroic confession of the love of God : " From my whole heart I confess the holy and adorable will of my God. . . . O my God, Thou willest it and I will it too, even if I suffer." " The blow is truly hard and difficult, but the hand that gave it is sweet and fatherly, therefore I kiss it and love it with my whole heart. I bow my head and incline my heart to His most holy will which with all my weak strength I honour and adore."

(iv) AGAINST HOLY INDIFFERENCE

(a) Holy Indifference and Quietism

If one looked at the history of ideas one could question whether the doctrine of St. Francis de Sales was not the precursor of Quietism which was later condemned by the Church. The Quietistic authors themselves had certainly often tried to justify their doctrine through allusion to Francis, Madame de Chantal, and Teresa. There certainly does exist something in common between the view of these three saints. Since 1606 the Baroness kept up a lively correspondence with the Carmelites at Dijon, whose prioress at that time was Ann of Jesus, the most treasured pupil of St. Teresa, her " daughter and crown ". In this way Madame de Chantal learned to know and to love Teresian mysticism. Francis did not like these mystical inclinations at first, but in order to do justice to the spiritual requirements of the Baroness, he began to study the writings of Teresa himself. He found a line of thought which corresponded with his own inclinations and, by incorporating it into his own system, he introduced a new element into the opulence of his thought, and also into his way of directing souls. In 1612 he gave the Baroness permission to repeat the Teresian prayer which is called the "prayer of quiet". This innovation on his part certainly did not occur until after 1611.

We must admit that if we take the words of this prayer out of their context and compare them superficially with various phrases of Quietistic literature, a certain impression of similarity could well emerge. Here as there we have the renunciation of individual activity, we have the "sleeping in the arms of Providence", the "glad will", even the indifference to the extent of renouncing eternal blessedness if God so wished. This similarity is explained if we realise that two systems, however differently they may develop, if they have the same basis, must have certain similar traits. Both systems, the Salesian and the Quietistic, aim at carrying through the theocentric conception of life to its logical conclusion—the highest possible love of God. Both systems recognise the counterpart to concentration as being the renunciation of all earthly cravings and the indifference with regard to all earthly things. But herein lies the error of Quietism, for it over-exaggerates this idea even so far as to contradict various truths of faith and reason—an error into which the saints I have mentioned never fell. Teresa, for example, had declared that the mystical union of the soul left the soul "so completely in the arms of God that she could suffer no pain if God wanted to send her to hell, so long as she knew that He desired it". Francis took over these thoughts and built them into his system, whose base is the doctrine of holy indifference. The indifferent soul, he declares, is so determined to conform to the divine pleasure "that—if we want to give an impossible example—it would sacrifice its blessedness and suffer damnation if it thought that damnation were more pleasing to God than salvation ".[1] This is intended only to serve as an example of unreserved surrender to God, as of course Francis knew very well that the will to salvation is placed in every man by God and neither should nor could be rejected. Quietism seriously preached an absolute acquiescence in one's own damnation as the peak of perfection. The idea that longing for one's own salvation lessened the perfect love of God was not new, for in patristic writings we find traces of it. Scholasticism repelled this error, but in the Seventeenth Century the exaggeration was unearthed and carried to its limit—the belief that a pure love of God would concur in one's own damnation. So, for instance, thinks Fénelon : " the soul brings the absolute sacrifice of its own salvation in eternity because this impossible event appears to it possible and actual . . . the spiritual director can allow the soul a simple consent to the loss of its own salvation and to its own damnation ".

In this assertion there lies a row of errors. The conception of good and God's will to save is practically denied ; the natural disposition of man is misunderstood and the essence of eternal punishment falsely conceived. Because if God were to find pleasure in the suffering of His creatures he could never be described as " Love ", and He would neither merit nor obtain such a heroic love on the side of the creature. A man who freely agreed to his own damnation against every instinct of self-assertion must be out of his mind. But a hell—and here lies the core of the whole extravagance—in which the soul lived in union with God would be no hell. Francis once declared : " Paradise would be there in the midst

[1] *Œuvres*, Vol. V, p. 122.

of all the torments of hell if the love of God were there." [1]
The Popes Innocent XI and Innocent XII condemned
the theory as " presumptuous, scandalous, and errone-
ous ". Francis's rhetorical comparison has nothing in
common with this exaggerated nonsense.

A similar conception is shown in the doctrine of the
renunciation of personal activity. St. Teresa describes
how the soul in the mystical union with God finds itself
as " in a condition of sleep ". In this observation she is
in agreement with Augustine, Bernard, and other mystics.
Francis declares : " To go into the presence of God and
to remain in the presence of God . . . are two different
things." To go into the presence of God needs a greater
or less great effort. One can remain with God, however,
insomuch as one contemplates Him or speaks with Him,
without any personal activity ; one can remain with Him
like a statue in a niche, like a bird in its nest, like a child
at the breast of its mother, like the apostle John at the
heart of Jesus. [2]   Francis knows how to treasure the joys
which result from such repose in God. He desires that
one should remain in such repose, like Mary who sat at
the feet of Jesus and not like Martha who was up and
busy. In this condition of repose, according to Francis,
the soul eliminates all inclinations to virtue and the
realisation of it. The will is as though dead. It renounces
all effort the nearer it is to God. Why ? Because it is so
deeply bound with God. " The seaman rests when he
arrives in a harbour," declares Peter of Alcantara. The
soul no longer experiences the desire to increase the
intensity of its union with God—that would be impossible ;
but it wishes to heighten the purity of the surrender.

[1] *Œuvres*, Vol. XV, p. 222.
[2] *Œuvres*, Vol. XXI, p. 96.

" It only fears that the union may not be as pure, simple and attentive as love would wish." Therefore it throws off all other pleasures so as to belong uniquely to the divine pleasure. But " one cannot long remain denuded of every inclination ", and therefore the soul will forthwith " re-clothe itself with the inclinations to virtue which it had resigned ".[1] The condition of quiet involves no cessation of individual activity but the form of the activity is changed. The soul does not press forward but remains where it is, which is the best possible place for it. It listens to the divine love with the most intense attention. Francis therefore declares that " there is never so much love in our will as when it dies to itself ". But love is a movement of the will ; and therefore the highest love involves the greatest activity. This is given with the attainment of the goal, the union with the beloved. On the summit of mystical communion with God the soul will gaze on God with blessed joy and with the greatest attention, but precisely because of this concentration it will abandon every activity so that, seen from outside, all the forces of the soul appear to sleep.

Quietism falls into error again by exaggeration. To the Quietists the inactivity of the soul appeared as the necessary condition for God's activity. " Natural activity is the enemy of grace," declares M. Molinos. The practical consequence of this error was the renunciation of the struggle against temptations, of religious practices and good works, of prayer and communion, and hence the renunciation of any progress in the religious life. Molinos, for instance, affirms, that in twenty-two years he had found " no adequate material for absolution ". Madame Guyon thinks : " These souls can hardly confess

[1] *Œuvres*, Vol. V, pp. 149, 161 *sq.*, 295.

for they do not know what they should accuse themselves of . . . they can discover nothing in themselves ". This naturally encourages a considerable laxity in the field of conscience, and a sugary blessedness of feeling becomes a substitute for ethical fact. In 1687 and 1699 the Church condemned these errors.

St. Francis de Sales never taught this false Quietism. He always represented the activity of the love of God. " Nothing," he emphasises in a letter of 1620, " nothing conduces so much to the realisation of the good as the heavenly love of God ; as long as we are in this world we can only love in that we do the good, for our love must be active." [1] This activity is always necessary, for our whole life stands under the shadow of the Fall. Again and again the inclination of fallen nature moves towards evil. " In this life, it is always necessary for us to purify ourselves . . . for our self-love keeps on causing us to fall back into imperfection." [2] " Life is a ceaseless battle against our inclinations " and " without a struggle no victory, without a victory no reward." [3] Yes, Francis is convinced that even in the high paths of life one must retain a rightful servile fear before God. " Even when the servant of God enjoys the rest and sweetness of divine love, he should never abandon fear before divine justice." Admittedly, at the time when he wrote the *Introduction* Francis had placed more emphasis on the " effective or active ", but with the composition of the *Traitté* the emphasis was more on " affective love ", *i.e.*, the mystical union of love of the soul with God. But he never forgot the necessity of a continuous striving upwards. He

---

[1] *Œuvres*, Vol. XIX, p. 250.
[2] *Œuvres*, Vol. IX, p. 16.
[3] *Œuvres*, Vol. XV, p. 247 ; Vol. XVII, p. 161.

himself has characterised the ideal which inspired the last ten years of his life with the words : " It is a great grace to combine the active with the passive and to go from one to the other ". [1]

Francis's words could only become suspicious when inexperienced hands took them out of their context and, by separating them from his complete system, converted them into a radical Quietism. Unfortunately Francis had bad luck in his followers. His exhortations that holiness and culture should be united in life—let us call this the ideal of the *Introduction*—was defaced by fools who said " how can one be a good Catholic without knowing different perfumes from one another ? " And his holy mysticism—the fundamental thesis of the *Traitté*—was exaggerated by his followers or distorted to mean a comfortable blessedness of feeling. But Francis's affirmations had a very different meaning. He was a practical man, and he always wanted to see practical efforts being made by his pupils. He said : " Holy resignation and holy indifference . . . require effort ". [2] It is in no way easy to educate the soul to these lofty ideals, in fact we might say that only a very healthy soul summoning all its strength can achieve holy indifference in life.

If we apply Francis's doctrine of repose in God to our own time, we see that it goes against all those active Catholics who overload themselves with so much work for the Kingdom of Christ in this world that they can no more find time for the cultivation of the Kingdom of God in their own hearts. It is directed against those representatives of the ascetical method who think that they can gain salvation only by disturbance and activity ; and

[1] *Œuvres*, Vol. V, p. 299 ; Vol. XIX, p. 53.
[2] *Œuvres*, Vol. V, p. 118.

therefore God's voice can never become words. Forced by the scheme of their method these people have always something or other to do, and if their director advises a dialogue between the soul and God it will be a monologue. They are like those people who always have to make speeches and who can never listen. The joyful lingering with God and the values derived from it are lost. St. Teresa referred to this error when she said : " Such souls think that they oughtn't to keep Sunday at all, or to rest one moment from work. It appears to them as so much waste of time. But I hold it as a great gain."

Francis, moreover, is hostile to the enemies of this ascetical exaggeration—namely those higher souls who are tired of vocational work in the world and seek the religious life so as to play the part of the child in the lap of its mother or a sleeping John on the breast of Jesus, and declare that this exceptional state is their perpetual one.

Francis's doctrine of repose in God has its main antagonists in the modern exaggeration of work and achievement which tries to enslave the whole of mankind. Many bow down to this idol of their own will, while others are forced to by the necessity of their professional position and are to be pitied. Of course, we praise the moral worth of vocational work, and consider it in no way as harmful ; it is a God-willed garden in which we should mature for eternity. Francis de Sales has stated this very clearly, and also our duty to serve the commonweal as much as is in our power.

The fact that we are in the world obliges us not only to work for the world but it also gives us a right to demand the forces necessary for the cultivation of our personality.

The Christian idea of life places the development of the ego before achievement. Development, however, never succeeds without the satisfaction of our natural requirements. We therefore desire a certain time for spiritual progress whether it is formation of the understanding, cultivation of the will or development of the heart. And because man was created by God and for God he requires this possibility in the religious sphere more than in the world. But in the religious sphere, besides our energetic struggle after union with God, the joyous experience of the divine gift has also its high meaning, because not only do we surrender ourselves to God but God gives Himself to us ; not the deed alone but also the repose and joy in God have therefore their special value. The final words of St. Francis de Sales—" combine the active with the passive "—points out to the saints of our time the right synthesis. Martha and Mary should go together. Active and contemplative life, asceticism and mysticism, vocational work and religious effort should go hand in hand. That is the demand of our time. It is especially true for priests and lay-apostles, for without this combination " we will achieve nothing for others, and harm ourselves ", as P. Lallemant (died 1634) declared.

(b) Holy Indifference and Stoicism

A second criticism of Francis's doctrine is expressed in the question : could not holy indifference be called a pursuit of stoical apathy ? The ethic of the Stoa began with the maxim : life in accord with nature is life in accord with reason. From this truth, however, the further consequences were drawn that virtue is the only true good and is enough in itself for holiness. In that every man can live in accordance with reason, which is synonymous with virtue, every man has it in his heart to become happy. But the stream of life which flows round us bringing us gifts and robbing us of possessions, is quite a different thing. All human unhappiness is caused by the logical error of considering accidents over which we have no control as values, and as a result our heart becomes dependent on transient things. The true philosopher strives primarily for the right valuation of things. Life and health, family and friends, honour and wealth, are in reality not goods ; death and sickness, the loss of those dear to us, degradation and poverty, are not real evils. Virtue is the only good, vice is the only evil. From this basic principle the wise man determines his attitude to the world. He knows that every inclination to some earthly thing or other causes a yearning for its possession and a dread of its loss. As, however, all earthly things are not in our control, we must necessarily become unhappy in the inevitable changing accidents of fate. Therefore the wise man frees himself from the chains of yearning, pleasure, fear and sadness, and liberates himself from all the tendencies which bring about a love for these trivialities. He is not satisfied with ruling and moderating the passions, as Plato and Aristotle advised, for these experiences are an evil and a moderated evil is still an evil. He suppresses the notion of the tendency itself and kills it at birth. " The peripatetics measure, but we eradicate, the passions," said Seneca. The real stoic educates his soul to passionlessness, to apathy. At a comfortable distance he sits on a secure bank and lets the stream of life ripple past his unfeeling and indifferent eyes. In this cold detachment and balance the stoics saw the essence of perfection and the basis of a happy life.

Undeniably and in spite of all its exaggerations against nature, there is a certain value in this view of life. There were lofty ambitions and great pains were taken to attain them. Severe asceticism was practised; for instance, Seneca examined his conscience every evening and gave himself four days' exercise per month. It is quite understandable that youthful Christianity, in its attempt to draw pagan philosophy into its service, readily seized on the writings of the Stoics. Tertullian, as an instance, speaks of " our Seneca ". An unknown cleric published Epictetus's *Handbook of Morality*, with a few alterations, as a school-book for Christian morality. His maxim *Abstine et sustine* (Renounce and endure) has found a lasting home in Christian asceticism. Clement of Alexandria asserts that Christ experienced no passion, and therefore every Christian should educate himself to apathy. Oriental monasticism sought to realise this ideal, and the West soon followed in its turn. Jerome wishes instincts to be done away with, and Cassian considers them as the demon against whom one should fight.

But with all these splendid theories and practical efforts we ought not to forget that the fruit of Stoic apathy was nothing but a weary resignation. Marcus Aurelius, the ruler of the world, had no plan for improving the world, but instead he surveyed mankind disapprovingly and yet hopelessly. Indifference led to passive resistance against the on-rushing of fate, and the killing of our instincts led to the death of living effort. Fatalism and Quietism were the result. Thus it was with the decline of the ancient world, and with the new version of these exaggerated ideas which came in with the Seventeenth Century. One can never wrest the essential ingredients of human nature from the human breast without being punished.

St. Francis de Sales was fully conscious of this. It was God Who had placed the passions and instincts in man. Hence, as St. Augustine said, " the citizens of the Holy City of God will feel fear and yearning, pain and joy, as long as they journey in this world. He Himself, the sovereign King of this city, experienced fear and yearning, pain and joy, to the extent of weeping, trembling and sweating blood ".[1] In Jesus's love for mankind we see the rush of the affections. " He shows a wonderful tenderness for little children, whom He took in His loving arms as He embraced them ; similarly He loved Martha, Mary, and Lazarus, for whom He wept." [2]

The affections belong to human nature and were created following the prototype of Christ's humanity. The formation of personality does not therefore consist in eradicating the passions but in integrating them into the human microcosm. The will, the king of the inner world, " should subject all these passions to the spirit, and the spirit to God. Ruled and directed thus, the passions are good, and as they come into the service of justice and virtue, they assume the character of virtues ".[3] That is true even of the most doubtful of all passions, anger. " This is a powerful, bold and enterprising servant and achieves much ; but because it is so strong, oppressive, unreflective and stormy, it usually fails to achieve good without at the same time perpetrating some evil." But in spite of all " it is a help . . . which grace can put into the service of zeal for the carrying out of its intentions ". " It is a dangerous help . . . but in desperate circumstances one must call out all auxiliaries

---

[1] Œuvres, Vol. IV, p. 31.
[2] Œuvres, Vol. V, p. 231.
[3] Œuvres, Vol. IV, p. 33 ;   Vol. V, p. 311.

in defence against a fault." [1]   Because of his conviction
of the justification and worth of the passions and affections
Francis condemns the Stoical attitude. "The Stoics
were very wrong in their assertion that a wise man
should eliminate all his passions. . . . They boasted that
they were exalted above passions, that they were people
without fear, without sadness, without anger, immovable
and unchangeable, but in reality they were subject to
confusion, unrest, impetuosity and other movements of
the senses." [2]   The statements of Aulus Gellius, Tacitus,
and Augustine testify to it. Vain desire for notoriety was
the motive of their long but empty words, and vanity was
the principal motive of their strivings towards virtue. In
these points Francis agrees with Mommsen's severe
definition of the Stoics as "swaggering and tedious
Pharisees".

"It is a great folly," declares the saint, "to want to be
wise in an impossible way. The Church has condemned
the folly of this unwisdom which certain conceited hermits
wanted to establish as wisdom." [3]   And Francis often
admits that he sees in this absence of affection nothing
noble, but rather a miserable stunting of human nature.
"That imagined sensitiveness of many people who do
not want to believe that man is man seems to me a
phantom of the brain. I do not love the souls who care
for nothing and face all the happenings of the world
unmoved. They do that only out of frailty and heartless-
ness and in consequence of contempt for the good as well
as for the evil." But, Francis goes on, those souls who
have given themselves over entirely to the will of God

[1] *Œuvres*, Vol. V, p. 219.
[2] *Œuvres*, Vol. IV, p. 30 ; Vol. V, pp. 270, 273.
[3] *Œuvres*, Vol. IV, p. 31.

and therefore remain indifferent must give thanks to the divine majesty, "for it is one of the greatest gifts ".[1] Here Francis publicly places the doctrine of indifference in direct contrast with Stoical apathy. The essential difference lies in this : The Stoa demands the death of affections, whereas Francis desires only to abolish the narrowing of spiritual freedom by the pressure of worldly affections. In *Faust* Goethe depicts the tension in the human breast : the higher soul " raises itself by force from the dust ", while the lower, " in powerful lust of love, embraces the world ". It is this clinging to the earth that Francis wishes to destroy root and branch, but the life of the affections should remain intact. Towards the end of the *Traitté* Francis shows us what he means by the indifference of the will with regard to fear and courage. When calamity threatens, he says, the soul speaks to God : " Thou willest, O Lord, that I should dread so that I may find the appropriate precautions to evade this disaster. I will do so, O Lord, because it is pleasing to Thee ". But if the soul has done all that it can to evade the threatening evil, it should pray peacefully : " Lord I am Thine ; deliver me if it so pleases You, but whatever may come I accept it, because it will come by Thy will ". Thus Francis saw that the instinct of fear inspires defence and the energy to act, and he knew very well the importance of these instincts and never desired to rob himself of them. Yet high above them soars the will to accept God's wishes without reserve. This will lays its hand on the unsteady heart, and the lower love bows down to the higher. So the will to holy indifference plays the part in religious life that the alchemists hoped the Philosopher's Stone would in the

[1] *Œuvres*, Vol. XIV, pp. 82, 163.

physical. " O holy Alchemy, O divine powder of meta-morphosis," cries Francis enthusiastically, " that converts all the metals of our passions, instincts and emotions into the purest gold of heavenly love." [1]

Thus we see that what Francis understands by indifference is nothing to do with the apathy of the Stoa nor the static rest of Quietism. Admittedly it is difficult to see how one is to conceive his indifference—how he intends that we should stand *vis-à-vis* with our friends and spouses, free from binding affections and yet loving them with great tenderness. We recognise that Francis, as a saint, must desire the concentration of all affection on God ; but we equally understand that as a humanist, and especially as a representative of the humanist-religious synthesis, he will renounce none of the noble life-values. How then is the union of this apparent contradiction going to be achieved ?

(v) HOLY INDIFFERENCE AND AFFECTION

It is an old Christian doctrine, and St. Thomas has propounded it, that the love of God has as general object God, and as immediate object the highest good ; but at the same time it embraces all that is of God, *i.e.*, its own ego and all the rest of mankind. " Why do we love God ? " asks St. Francis de Sales, and answers, " because He is the highest infinite good. Why do we love ourselves in the love of God ? Because we are God's image and likeness, and because all men possess the same dignity and are holy and living images of God." To love " means to love God for love of Himself, and to love the creature through the love of God. The true love of our neighbour

[1] *Œuvres*, Vol. V, p. 313.

is the love of God in man ". " Why," he asks, " did
Raguel embrace the young Tobias as soon as he introduced himself as the son of his cousin ? Raguel explains
to Tobias : ' Certainly not because thou art an excellent
young man, for that I know not yet ; but because thou
art the son and the replica of thy father, a quite excellent
man '." The reason for the affectionate meeting was thus
not the personality of the young man, but the fact that
he was the son of the old Tobias. And in the same way
it is not the personal qualities of one's neighbour but the
divine element in him that is the object and motive of the
Christian love of one's neighbour. It requires no personal
connection, no great knowledge of the other, but merely
the consciousness that all men are children of God Whom
we love. Thus originally the love of one's neighbour
should not be an immediate relationship between self
and self, but the stream of love mounts first to God and
then flows out from God over His creation. Therefore
Jesus's first commandment is to love God and immediately joined on to it is the love of one's neighbour, for,
as He declares, they are one and the same thing. Hence
St. John says : " If someone says I love God, and hates
his brother, he is a liar." Only " if we love one another
God remains in us, and His love in us is perfect ". " Who
loves not, knows not God." Augustine shows this unity
of love when he writes : " through this love we love one
another. Through this love we love God. We would
not love one another with a true love if we did not love
God, so everyone loves his neighbour as himself if he loves
God ". The separation of loving one's neighbour from
the love of God results in the mutilation of the love of
God. " It is," declares Francis, " one and the same love
which produces the acts of love of God and of one's

neighbour . . . it is the same love which elevates us to the union of the soul with God and leads to a living community with our neighbour. The love of God does not only command, but creates the love of our neighbour." [1] Francis asserts " God loves all that is and hates nothing of that which He has created ". " Let us love God and we will love everything else." [2]

But how about our particular affections ? Is our love of God's creatures which overflows from our love of Him a purely spiritual love, an act of the will dictated by judgment and understanding ? Scholastic theology, asserting that the soul possesses only the two powers of understanding and will, described the will as the bearer of love. Here emotion seems to be merely the companion of will in man's physical nature and the highest love need not necessarily express itself in an emotional way. If the spirit is depressed or disturbed then every perceptible emotion of love can be lacking, and yet a complete love of God can fill the soul. Because of this correct affirmation, the other truth was forgotten, that in normal circumstances a deep movement of the will has also a corresponding movement of the emotions, and that the true love of God must include the affections—because of the psychological unity in human nature—if the whole man is to love God with all his powers. And that is demanded clearly by Christ's principal commandment. Matthew, Mark, and Luke, who recount this sermon of Jesus, use the Greek expression $\dot{\alpha}\gamma\alpha\pi\alpha\nu$. The word refers to the higher purely spiritual love in contradistinction to $\phi\iota\lambda\epsilon\iota\nu$, which means a love based on natural attraction. The bearer of the higher love is the will, but when Christ

[1] Œuvres, Vol. V, pp. 204–206.
[2] Œuvres, Vol. IV, pp. 196 sq.

expressly says : " Thou shalt love the Lord thy God with thy whole heart, and thy whole soul, and thy whole mind, and thy whole strength," then it is obvious that He is not satisfied only with the love of the will but desires a love in which every human faculty takes part.

But unfortunately Christian people are all too ready to limit love to the act of will. Prayers, narrow and short, state what theological science demands from an act of perfect love and the life of the real affections lies fallow. Therefore these affections go their own way to objects perceptible by the senses, and the clash between higher and lower love, the love of the will and the love of the emotions, becomes tragically self-evident. So the life of many men degenerates into an eternal struggle against an enemy which one cannot slay and equally cannot befriend. The struggle usually ends in capitulation of the will to the emotions, and even if the negative exhortation " Thou shalt not " can hold the sensual urge in check, the positive value of the warm affections and the deep emotions is lost to religious life. To-day we see religious life becoming mere duty, a burden that one bears because one must. The decay of the proper feeling leads to a personal incompleteness, for the perfect Christian is, according to the prototype of Christ, the perfect man. This lack is the reason why that joy in the beautiful which usually inspires admiration and imitation in the onlooker, does not inspire self-willed men in spite of their recognised intellectual formation and æsthetically strict life. Do we not often hear the phrase : A holy man, but an unpleasant person ? The stunting of honourable manliness causes the word holiness to degenerate. We only have to ask our acquaintances if they are holy and they will reply : Holy ! let us rather say interested in religion. Thus to neglect the cultivation of the emotions is one of those streams of misfortune which retard the completion of the holy personality in us, robs it of its proselytising strength of attraction, and prejudices public opinion about becoming holy. Thus purely intellectual love is not enough for life nor for Christ's commandment.

Now St. Francis de Sales' characteristic observation of life showed him that love without deep affection was not true love. Humanistic psychology bears him out when he says : " a heart that has no movement, no emotion, no feeling, has no love. And conversely, a heart that has love must also have emotion and affection ". The love that glows with emotion is " the principle of a holy life ".[1]

We have seen already how Francis took pains to integrate the emotions into the love of God, and we will see how this idea culminates in the emotional conception of religious life on which his system is based. Francis's love of God is full of warmth, and it is this same love that extends over His whole creation. Consequently the love of the creature can also be deeply affectionate and a glance at his life shows that he loved his family and friends with the greatest tenderness.

Thus it is obvious that Francis is not on the side of those who eliminate all natural feelings, every joy in possession, and every sorrow over loss. The Gospels show clearly that Jesus's love for man was deep and warm and passionate. For example, Francis could not under-stand the sort of scriptural commentators who interpreted Christ's weeping at the tomb of Lazarus as caused by the thought that Lazarus was to re-enter the dangers and struggles of the world. He holds that sorrow about death

[1] Œuvres, Vol. V, p. 29.

is morally permitted. Though St. Augustine tried to
stifle his inner emotion by force when his mother died, he
considered the " short hour " which he spent in weeping,
though perhaps a little guilty, nevertheless pardonable.
Francis tells us quite openly of his deep affliction at the
death-bed of his mother. " I had the strength to give her
the last blessing, to close her eyes and her mouth, and to
give her a last kiss of peace at the moment of departure,
but then my heart broke, and I wept more than I had
ever wept since belonging to the Church, but my tears
were without spiritual bitterness." The juxtaposition of
complete surrender to the divine will, and the burning
emotion of pain, is often shown in Francis's letters. For
instance, when he received the message that his brother
was dying he wrote : " My heart is certainly deeply
moved, but I pray with my whole strength to God . . .
yea, Eternal Father, while it is so pleasing before Thee ".
And at the news of his death he declared : " He is
happy, I know, but I cannot help crying over him ".
" I cannot dismiss the emotions of pain which nature
moves in me." [1]

Francis did not like the unnatural hardening of the
heart against sorrow which we find in some saints. For
example, St. Angela of Foligno declared that the loss of
her family had been " a great consolation " to her. A
similar attitude is shown in the letters of St. Antoninus,
who once consoled a bewailing woman by affirming that
the death of her child and husband meant a lessening of
otherwise necessary works and troubles. He commanded her to pray : " I thank Thee Lord that Thou
hast made me free so that I can serve Thee entirely ".
Francis declares that such rigours on the part of some

[1] *Œuvres*, Vol. XIV, p. 262.

saints are " more an object of admiration than imitation ".
He sees the religious worth in reading about such saints,
but he himself does not share in their conception. He
once praised a young widow for her complete surrender
to God's will, but he especially emphasised the fact that :
" She showed this holiness in the midst of her tears and
sorrow ". He admires the combination of both most of
all : " Such a love for the husband who has gone and such
a resoluteness for enduring the bitterness of his departure ! " [1]

Francis himself weeps with those who weep. " My
heart," he writes in a letter, " sympathises deeply with
the joys and pains of my beloved daughters." When
little Charlotte, Madame de Chantal's ten-year-old
daughter, died, his first thought of consolation was :
" Our poor little Charlotte is blessed in having left this
world before it touched her." But immediately he goes
on : " Ah, one must weep a little, for have we not a
human heart and a human nature ? Why then should
we not weep a little over our departed since the Spirit of
God does not only allow it but even advises it ".[2] Francis
expressly declares that weeping is allowed, and as proof
he refers not only to the natural inclination of human
nature but also to the words of Holy Scripture : " Weep
over someone dead ". The reason why Francis was at
such pains to emphasise something which to us seems
obvious is because his correspondent was Madame de
Chantal who, in her striving for holy indifference, was
often inclined to try and crush the natural impulses of
motherly love. The Baroness was in no way that unfeeling
woman that so many people have liked to imagine on

---

[1] Œuvres, Vol. III, p. 108 ; Vol. XVIII, pp. 19, 22.
[2] Œuvres, Vol. XIV, p. 264 ; Vol. XVIII, p. 15.

account of her entering a convent in spite of her little children. The facts are that the youngest girl was taken to the convent with her to be educated, the eldest daughter had already married, and the education of the eldest son, who was the main opposer of his mother's departure, lay in the hands of his grandfather, the president of Dijon. At one time Francis thought that the Baroness was carrying holy indifference too far, and thus he put a bridle on her enthusiasm. When the young Baron once came to visit his mother, Francis—thinking that his reception would be very cool—wrote : " How sorry I am not to be able to witness the caresses which Celse Bernine will receive from a mother who has become unfeeling against all the natural instincts of a mother's love ! I believe in fact that the caresses will be very brief. Ah ! no, my dear daughter, do not be so cruel ! Show him joy on this visit, this poor, young Celse Bernine ! " [1]

Thus Francis, in his direction of souls and in his own life, works on the assumption that perfect indifference and affectionate love can and should go hand in hand. There is one more question, however : How is an outlet formed for this psychical experience in which the heart frees itself from all creatures and nevertheless returns to a warm love for the same creatures ?

At first the soul concentrates all its forces, without any exception or any reservation, on God, the unique goal of its being. Freely it soars up to that highest peak of perfection where God alone stands in overpowering greatness before its eyes. There the earth disappears from sight, earthly goods have no more charm, and the heart has become indifferent with regard to all earthly things. But man finds in God the creator of all true, good,

[1] *Œuvres*, Vol. XVI, p. 38.

and beautiful things in the world, the creator of his own being, Who has ordered human inclinations towards created values. Hence the soul descends once more the Jacob's ladder of love. Once again it loves home, forests, flowers, family, friends, art and science, but with a new love—no longer because the earthly ego hankers and then enjoys selfish satisfaction, but rather for the will of the most beloved Father in Heaven Who has created all these good things and now wills that His child should have joy in them.

Francis once used the expression : The soul cast off all its inclinations and stood naked before God. But now it clothes itself once more with the " earlier inclinations ", —parents, home, father, house and friends, but they are " other, new " inclinations. For this new love is born again from the spirit of the Our Father, " that the name of Our Father should be hallowed, His kingdom extended and His good pleasure satisfied ".[1]

The personality of our saint shows his ideal translated into reality. " I believe," he once wrote, " that all, with the exception of God, is nothing to me any longer : but in Him and for Him I love more tenderly than ever what I love." Once he declared to Madame de Chantal : " Nothing or God ! because all that is not God is either nothing or less than nothing. So remain completely in Him, my dear daughter, and pray that I too remain there utterly. And therein we should love one another mightily, my daughter, for we can never love too much or even enough. What joy to love without fear of exaggeration ! But there is never the least to fear when one loves in God ".[2] Thus we see how indifference and deep

---

[1] Œuvres, Vol. V, p. 162.
[2] Œuvres, Vol. XIV, p. 230 ; Vol. XV, p. 17.

love are bound together in Francis's soul, and the act of
love to a friend follows directly from the act of love to
God.   We see, too, the nature of the love between St.
Francis de Sales and Madame de Chantal, which has
been the cause of so much misunderstanding.

Francis is so removed from those spirits who ruled Port-
Royal several decades later !   There, every feeling of the
heart savoured of fleshly concupiscence.   A cold detachment and restrained friendship was required.   Francis, on
the contrary, praises the religious value of holy friendship
and intercedes for affection in human relationships.   It is
certainly not the meaning of religion to try and crush the
noble inclinations given us by God, but rather to sanctify
them through identifying them with the love of God and
thus bringing them to completion.

PART FOUR

LOVE AND ASCETICISM

(i) ASCETICISM

ST. PAUL besought the newly converted Ephesians to
" lay off the old man according to the earlier dispensation
. . . and draw on the new man who is created according
to God ". Many ascetics considered the laying-off of the
old man as the essence of a renaissance to a new life and,
because of this over-valuation, their lives were entirely
taken up with the business of throwing-off. The renunciation of life-values, the throwing-off of all life-desires and
the limiting of life-necessities to the minimum, seemed to
them the core of all perfection. There is a tendency in
this direction in Christian antiquity ; the ideal of
Diogenes, the doctrines of the Stoic, and the new Pytha-
gorean and Neo-Platonic ethic did not, of course, found
Christian asceticism but cast their shadow over its development. They hoped thereby to gain support for their
philosophy and a valuable means of propaganda in the
cultured world. But the grafted shoot was essentially
foreign to Christianity in some respects, and therefore it
could not develop but had to dry up again. The
enthusiasm of St. Clement of Alexandria for freedom from
needs, and his declaration : " God has given us the right
of enjoyment but only within the confines of the necessary ", betray the presence of this grafted shoot in

Christian asceticism. The great theologians, however, have always tried to remove an over-valuation of ascetical abstinence. " It serves no purpose," declares St. Francis de Sales, " if one denies oneself and thereby remains at a standstill. The old philosophers achieved this self-renunciation in a way worthy of admiration, but it did not help them. One must renounce the earthly man so as to strengthen the heavenly man." It is, of course, valuable to mortify one's lower nature and so struggle against one's self-love.[1] But the measure of necessary renunciation and the field in which it must be practised should be uniquely conditioned by the object to be attained : that of finding a free way to higher love. One may move the mistletoe which is parasitic on trees, or cut off the wild shoots on the vine—Francis uses both these similes—but one should neither mutilate nor cripple nature herself. " I praise your method," declares Francis, " but it is not mine." [2] These words occur in the first letter of spiritual direction which Francis wrote after his return from Paris in 1602, and they are directed against a system of spiritual direction which wants to cut other souls to measure. If we look at Francis's own method, we can see that it is not his desire to mutilate nature. He wants no unnecessary or unnatural self-limitation. " Catharsis ", the purification of the life of the soul, is merely presupposition and not the essence of perfection. Asceticism is not an end in itself, but a means to an end. It is precisely justified and necessary in so far as it removes the obstacles and difficulties which oppose a happy unfolding of the love of God. If it steps beyond this, harms one's health or interferes with any force of life

[1] *Œuvres*, Vol. XVII, p. 160.
[2] *Œuvres*, Vol. XII, p. 148.

which could become fruitful in the service of love, then it should be rejected as wrong.

(ii) POSITIVE OVER NEGATIVE

A further characteristic peculiarity of Salesian asceticism is revealed by the method of curing evil inclinations. A glance at the method of curing physical unhealthiness shows us two possibilities : removal of the ailing organ or the cure of the source of the illness. Contemporary medical science allows the removal of parts of the body only in the last resort, for the result is obviously a maimed man. In the spiritual field such encroachments were even more doubtful. The Stoics brought about their cures by force, and Francis, as we have already seen, was in no agreement with this. A removal of a spiritual faculty is impossible, but such faculties can be repressed, and if this is done too strongly a dangerous deterioration of spiritual life will result. Just as in physical life some cure of the root of the ill must be attempted, so in spiritual life. Medical science differentiates between two methods, homeopathy and allopathy. In Francis's time these two methods contrasted with one another, and the saint referred to them so as to illustrate his idea about spiritual cures. " The Methodics among doctors live by the maxim : A thing is cured by its opposite. The Spagirics, on the contrary, insist that a thing is cured by its like." " Similarly," declares Francis, " we fight our passions either by opposing them with opposite passions, or by concentrating them on higher movements of the same kind." For example, one can overcome the longing for wealth and transitory joys either by disdaining them or by longing for permanent joys, and one can fight the vain hope and trust in human kindness through opposing considerations. " O, foolish man ! on what basis do you build your hope ? Do you not see that the great man on whom you put your trust stands as near to death as you yourself ? Do you not know the inconstancy, weakness, and wretchedness of the human spirit ? To-day a heart belongs to you, to-morrow it will belong to another. On what then is your hope based ? I can offer resistance to this hope in opposing to it a more solid hope —hope in God, my soul ! No one has yet hoped in Him and come to harm ! " [1]

With the first method, therefore, the soul endeavours to reduce the devoted object to shreds and thus acquires a feeling of scorn and antipathy for it. With the second method there is no direct attack, for the soul attains to such a powerful trust in God that every longing for human help appears as idle and is therefore abandoned. The stars, declares Francis, disappear when a thick mist hangs in front of them ; they also disappear when bright sunlight is in front of them. This obscuring of the sensually alluring object Francis achieves by outshining the object with the radiant illumination of the true good. Side by side with the checking of dangerous inclinations he places the cultivation and strengthening of the good ones ; therefore, beside negative asceticism he places the positive development of noble striving, and beside direct fighting through attack he places an indirect fighting through turning away from the enemy and busying the forces of the soul with better things. With the consequent concentration of all knowledge and effort on the ethical ideal there necessarily comes a weakening of evil inclinations, for concentration and indifference are inseparable com-

---

[1] *Œuvres*, Vol. V, pp. 311 *sq*.

panions. Francis wants the soul to be entirely absorbed in thinking of God and filled with an inner love of God, as he is convinced that in such a way all earthly things will lose their dangerous charm and every evil inclination will fade away. Bossuet took over Francis's idea as his pupil, Madame Courineau, shows us when she says : " He was not of the opinion that one could completely annihilate the passions through their opposite . . . rather one must change the object of one's passions through elevating them ". Psychology and the observation of life show the rightness and usefulness of both methods. Francis studied the Gospels from this point of view and came to the conclusion that our Lord employed both methods in his spiritual healing—the first, *i.e.*, the direct fighting of an affection through its opposite, when He contrasts joy with sadness : " Woe to ye who laugh, for ye will weep hereafter," and the second, *i.e.*, the elimination of the lower desires by attaching them to the highest objects when he places a higher object against a lower : " Be not glad that evil spirits are subject to you, but because your names are written in Heaven ". Similarly Jesus suppresses the fear of men through the fear of God. " Fear not those who kill the body, but fear him who can kill the soul."

Both methods are good and serviceable. The asceticism of the previous age gave us the first, but Francis laid special value on the second, which owes its development to him. The further development proceeds, the more the positive method takes precedence over the negative. God's wisdom demanded that the people of the Old Testament should struggle against sin. In the New Testament, however, Christ, the divine Pedagogue—as Clement of Alexandria named him—laid stress on the

positive striving after higher virtues ; the " Blessed are
they " of the Sermon on the Mount is an appeal to positive
qualities. The depicting of justice as the basis of spiritual
selection presupposes positive achievement : " I was
naked and ye clothed me, I was hungry and ye gave me
to eat." Observation of life justifies the assumption that
the formation of the individual personality goes along the
same lines as the education of all humanity. The further
moral formation is developed, the more must asceticism
change over from negative to positive methods, until the
time comes when most men can no longer deal with their
faults through frontal attack but through the illumination
of the whole personality which causes the faults to
melt away like the last flecks of snow in the spring
sunshine.

Medical science of to-day is coming more and more to
recognise that it is the strength of life that overcomes
sickness. Consequently strengthening the life force is
more important than a special treatment of the evil that
is causing the trouble. Three hundred years before,
Francis had advocated the same opinion in the field of
moral doctoring. " Love is the life of the soul, as the soul
is the life of the body." [1] Full strength of love requires
perfection of the soul. A growth of love must therefore
lead to the health of the soul. Francis also mentions the
difficult points of moral education where it is not a matter
of conversion from sin but the continual formation of
religious men, not the negative " Thou shalt not " but
the positive " Thou shalt ". The majority of ethical
writers with Cassian at their head fixed their eyes rigidly
on sin ; the *age contra* (act against) became the cry of their
wisdom. But Francis's glance was not directed backwards

---

[1] *Œuvres*, Vol. XVII, p. 206

to sin, but forwards to union with God, and therefore the negative side of moral life, the struggle against sin, stands in the second place. A letter, written in the year 1613, clearly reveals Francis's opinion : " You must be intent upon this . . . to fight your evil inclinations through concentration on the higher virtues, through determination to be zealous, more attentive and more active in the practice of virtue. Mark these words : your sin derives from the fact that you fear vice more than you love virtue." [1] This spirit inspires Francis's writing and rules his whole spiritual direction. This basic attitude conditions the way in which he judges and forms the personality, and thus it is that he gives a more important place to looking outwards, and a less important place to examination of conscience than most doctors of the spiritual life.

(iii) ASCETICISM AND THE INNER LIFE

Francis's thought is governed by love, but love lives in the soul. Hence we get a further peculiarity of Salesian asceticism, which is that the formation of the saint must be carried on in the inner part of man. Already in October, 1604, Francis had said : " First the inner life must be set in order . . . and then we will set the outer life right, because such is the true and solid method ".[2] In the definitive edition of the *Introduction* he repeats this declaration and openly states : " So far as I am concerned, Philothea, I could never agree with the method of those who begin the formation of man with the outer posture of the body, the clothes and the hair. I believe

---

[1] *Œuvres*, Vol. XV, p. 358.
[2] *Œuvres*, Vol. XII, p. 342.

that one must begin within. ' Convert yourselves to me
out of your whole heart,' says God. My child, give your
heart ! For the heart is the source of all action . . .
surely he who has Jesus Christ in his heart has Him
forthwith in all his actions ".[1] Francis rejects the method
which seems always to be so popular, that of re-fashioning
the exterior life first and thence working backwards to the
soul. He looks on the formation of the outer life merely
as a consequence and expression of a reformed soul.
" The daughters of this congregation," he declares to
some nuns, " must let the outer be an overflowing from
the inner." " It is the inner man on which all my
thoughts concentrate." [2] Camus relates of him : " He
did not agree with those who begin the improvement
from outside so as . . . to make the way inwards ".
These are like painters who create nothing real but only
a deceptive image of reality. Whether this comparison
comes from Francis or from Camus unfortunately is not
known. From this standpoint Francis changes the various
methods put forward by traditional asceticism. Much
that had been put in the foreground he puts in the background, and drags forward what had been subordinate.
He enriches the usual doctrine of asceticism by new
thoughts, new acts, new practices and formulations.

The first element in religious formation is, according
to Francis, the decision to give oneself over entirely to
the love of God. This decision should be made by an
act of solemn consecration. This idea might have been
given to him by the consecration of priests and monks.
At St. Claude, where he took over the religious direction
of Madame de Chantal, he first put this idea of con-

[1] *Œuvres*, Vol. III, pp. 116 *sq.*
[2] *Œuvres*, Vol. VI, p. 13 ; Vol. XIII, p. 13.

secration into practice, and wrote to her : " Every year
we should celebrate the anniversary of our consecration
in some special way. I call this the day of our consecration because on it we consecrated ourselves entirely
to God ".[1]   The result was so successful that he recommended everybody to do the same thing, and he gives a
methodical instruction for this solemnity in the *Introduction*.
First of all, the soul prepares itself throughout a number
of days, and then baptises itself in a general confession,
so as " to renew its youth like an eagle ".[2]   Then follows
the solemn declaration of the " decision to belong entirely
to God, body, heart and soul ".   The conclusion is the
receiving of Holy Communion, which is like " a holy
seal " placed on the heart. With psychological acuteness
the saint advises this festive celebration of the new life.

Francis knows that even the holiest and most sincere
decisions tend to fade from the memory with the passage
of time. Hence he takes care that the remembrance of
the day of consecration shall never fade. He writes a
letter to an unknown correspondent as the anniversary
approaches : " This day is counted amongst the most
important of our life. O may it be reckoned as only less
important than the day of our baptism ! This day on
which we renewed our inner temple, on which we laid
the foundation stone of our salvation, the prognostication
of the holy and desired eternal glory ! The remembrance
of this day will not only make us joyful in this life but in
life everlasting ".[3] Francis tries to reawaken in the soul
the solemn feeling and holy enthusiasm of the day of
consecration, because he knows what value such festive

---

[1] *Œuvres*, Vol. XIII, p. 51.
[2] *Œuvres*, Vol. XII, p. 367.
[3] *Œuvres*, Vol. XIII, p. 242.

hours have in ordinary lives. The ancient Christians used to renew their confession of faith and baptismal vow every year on the anniversary of their baptism day, and so, according to Francis, should we.

This remembrance can be combined with a self-examination. Just as a man must wind up his watch regularly, and at least once a year take it to pieces and renew the worn-out parts, so also good resolutions need a frequent overhauling. Francis dedicates the fifth book of the *Introduction* to this annual renewal, when the self-examination is summed up in the question : " How is the condition of your heart with regard to God ? "

To-day we often pray : " O my God I love Thee above all things ". Thoughtful souls suspect the genuineness of this glib declaration and would like to obtain some confirmation of its truth. Augustine prepared several questions for self-analysis : " If God said : Thou shalt never see my face, but shall possess all earthly fortune, and what dost thou want more ? there would be the cry : Take all from me, but let me see thy face. But if God said : I will not damn thee to Hell, but I will remove my face from thee, and thou still saidst : Take all from me ! —then it would be really from the love of God ". Similarly Francis de Sales asks various questions of the soul : " Dost thou often think of God, and art thou joyful in the thought ? does the memory of God come to thee in the midst of this world and in the midst of trivialities ? " " And does thy heart turn joyfully to these happy thoughts as a bride who hastens to meet her husband returning home ? " [1] These are concise questions from which we can gauge fairly clearly what our attitude to God is. What do you think about most ? What do you think

[1] *Œuvres*, Vol. III, p. 346.

about when on a walk or when by yourself? Money,
work, enjoyment or God? and what makes you most
happy?—possessions, success, or the consciousness that
Christ is yours and you are His? Francis once saw a holy
picture of the Child Jesus standing over a heart. He saw
in that a symbol of the stability of the pure surrender of
the soul to God. It pleased him so much that the picture
was reproduced on the title-page of the *Traitté*. The
consciousness of belonging entirely to the Saviour should
be the source of our joy in life. If we can affirm that
such is the genuine attitude of our soul, then it is a proof
that we really love God.

It is our duty in life to cultivate this love and to increase
its intensity and activity. The sources of strong love are
concentration and holy indifference. Its opposite is the
love of oneself which must be overcome. The struggle
between love of God and love of oneself takes place
essentially in the inner part of man, and conquest over
our will leads to certain victory. " The coin with which
we must buy perfection is our self-will." [1] Francis
emphasises untiringly this spiritual asceticism. His
attitude here is like that of St. Augustine, the German
mystics of the Fourteenth Century and the Italian school
of the Sixteenth Century who similarly referred asceticism
to the inner world. The Spaniards also held this point
of view and St. Peter of Alcantara writes : " Our self-
will must die so that the will of God can live and rule in
us ". But like the other authors of this school he lays
great emphasis on physical mortification : First one
must practice self-discipline in the matter of food, drink,
clothes, abode, and all the requirements of this life ;
through genuflection, stretching out the arms, standing

[1] *Œuvres*, Vol. IX, p. 82.

upright or lying prostrate in prayer ; through scourging, hair-shirts, long fastings and nocturnal vigils. St. Francis de Sales lays considerably less emphasis on the chastisements of the body and other practices of external asceticism. His directions for life in the cloister show this clearly. In the autumn of 1602 he declared that poverty and the spirit of community in a convent are much more important than the questions as to whether one preferred " this or that mortification ", wore " this or that garment " or assumed this or that posture when praying. In 1605 he says in his proposals for the reform of Puits d'Orbe : " Not only will I not import any external austerity, but I will introduce a very great mildness ; for it is the life within with which my thoughts are concerned ". In 1609 he wrote to Madame de Chantal that in the planned new order of the *Visitation* the nuns should have " their feet well shod yet at the same time their hearts quite free from earthly considerations ". In the prefatory observation to the Rule of the order he goes directly against the idea that women should see the essence of sanctity in austerity, and should be " more intent in keeping their stomachs free from meat than their minds free from self-will ". Instead he forms the Constitution of the order on the basis of inner asceticism.[1] He writes : " *Moins de rigueur pour le corps—plus de douceur de cœur* " (Less rigour for the body—more gentleness of heart). It is true that he admits that a strict mode of life may be a valuable means of arriving at perfection and recommends " little practices of strictness " as the occasion arises.[2] But he does not introduce this into the constitution, though he does say : " Where the strictness

---

[1] *Œuvres*, Vol. XXV, pp. 13, 29.
[2] *Œuvres*, Vol. XXI, p. 7.

of physical mortification is lacking, one must by so much more possess perfection of spirit ". Francis consciously deviates from tradition, and it is understandable that the followers of the strict mediæval ideal should have directed their criticism against this new conception of the cloistered life. But Francis did not waver in his emphasis that " the spirit of mildness is so much the spirit of the Visitation that anyone who wants to introduce greater austerity . . . will immediately destroy its spirit ".

It was only at the very beginning of Francis's life as a leader that he recommended a scourging of " fifty to sixty strokes, or only thirty, according to physical condition ". In 1615 he said that he agreed that " the penitential shirt should be worn once a week ", but adds immediately " presuming that through this you are not too tired for more important practices, as is often the case ".[1] It is true that in 1604 he was of the opinion that " six hours' sleep seemed quite enough ",[2] but afterwards he repeatedly speaks of seven and eight hours' sleep, and rejects the exaggerated shortening of the night's rest, although in exceptional cases he counsels vigils by the Holy Sepulchre. Besides the harm done to the health through insufficient sleep, Francis says that " one is without strength throughout the whole of the following day " and that " the spirit of piety is stifled ". Similarly Francis opposes any exaggerated limitation of food and drink whereby one becomes " more weak than holy, more ill than mortified ".[3] Francis sees in some of the Fathers of the Desert who, under the influence of the old Platonic dualism, saw in the body the grave of the soul,

[1] Œuvres, Vol. XII, p. 357 ; Vol. XVII, p. 102.
[2] Œuvres, Vol. XII, p. 355.
[3] Œuvres, Vol. XII, p. 336.

neither a pledge of personal holiness, nor an elevation over earthly desires. The traditional temptations of many Fathers of the Desert justify his point of view. Neither does St. Francis agree with the view of St. Jerome who wanted a " daily fast " and " an ever hungry stomach " and recommended children never to eat to complete satiety. Francis frequently gives a dispensation from the ecclesiastical commandments to fast [1] because we need the little strength we have for those more important practices on which progress in religious life depends. Conserve your spiritual strength so as to serve God in the spiritual offices.

Francis is fully aware that great contemplation and prayers from the depths of the soul need energy. " It is a very good sign," he declares, " if a body becomes exhausted by it." Therefore he desires that the body should be attentively looked after through the right nourishment and revivifying sleep. " One must be very careful to do all that helps to keep us strong and fresh . . . for we have efforts to make to become holy and to achieve great things for God and our neighbour." [2] For the sake of these two main objects of living—which derive from Christ's chief commandment to love God and one's neighbour—Francis limits the chastisement of the body which until his time was so rigorous. But it is a great mistake to think that this was because he was a kindly and mild saint. He demands the highest achievement in our own personalities and for God's kingdom. Therefore he restrains any squandering of strength. He provided an inexhaustibly wide field for activity—in the mortification of the will and in holy indifference. He once declared

[1] Œuvres, Vol. XIII, p. 133 ; Vol. XIV, pp. 161, 270, 323.
[2] Œuvres, Vol. XVII, p. 9.

that the devil fears the mortification of our desires much more than the chastisement of the body.

(iv) PRAYER AND LOVE

Francis considered the different forms of prayer from the point of view of what most enkindles a love for God. Usually people distinguish between inner and oral prayer, according to whether the words are thought or spoken. Ascetically considered this distinction is unimportant, because the fact that the voice is added to the thought of the heart " neither increases nor decreases the effect of the prayer ". Luis of Granada declared " that between the two there is scarcely any difference ". Psychologically the advantage of oral prayer lies in the fact that spoken words are supposed to " awaken devotion and arouse the heart ".

More important is the distinction between set prayers which are written for us and our own formless prayers. For community prayer obviously the formulated prayers are needed, and no less obviously official services must ignore individual variations and use the universally valid prototypes of prayer. But in private devotion the soul ought to speak to God like a child to its father. Here the personal thought and feeling and its expression in self-invented formulæ takes the prominent place. The Prayer Book should only be used as a last resort so as to bridge over the deficiencies. Luis of Granada values the formulated prayer, too, as an " oral prayer ". He recommends this especially to beginners in the religious life, because here, as in nature, " the young and tender plant needs a support against which it can grow ". St. Teresa advises those souls who " cannot meditate by themselves " to make use of " a book so as to avoid aberration of thought ".

History shows that private prayer since the Fourth Century tended to use formulæ. St. Athanasius placed the Psaltery as the centre of the life of prayer, even private prayer. He was convinced that one found in the Psalms the best words for all occasions ; and so as to facilitate an appropriate use of the Psalms, he made a detailed register of possible requirements and the Psalms that corresponded to them. Thus we read : " If you see the arrogance of the masses and the prevalence of evil, flee to the Lord and recite the 11th Psalm. . . . If you suffer persecution recite the 3rd. . . . If you admire the order of creation say the 18th and 23rd . . . and if you observe how the Lord helps you and leads you, recite joyfully the 22nd. . . . If you have sinned and are repentant you will find words of confession in Psalm 50 . . . and if you wish to praise the Lord on His Feast Day you have the Psalms 80 and 94 ". For St. Athanasius therefore the indispensable basis of correct prayer lies in the Psalms. Learn the Psalms, he exhorts the Christian Virgins ; " the rising sun should see the Book of Psalms in your hand ". And, so that a formulated prayer may not degenerate into mere lip-work, he adds : " And you must think over the sense of each several word ". Oriental monasticism took over this view and later it penetrated to Western monasticism. St. Jerome demands that little girls should learn the Psalms by heart, and thus the Psalms became the set prayer book through which all could raise their hearts and feelings to God. The textual prayer therefore played the principal part in mediæval devotion.

The result was an absolute plethora of written prayers, and with this came the danger of mechanical recitation.

People saw the progress of religious life in the increase of the number of prayers written. Quantity got the upper hand of quality, and we find it recorded that Macarius said twenty-four prayers on the way to a small grotto and twenty-four on the way back. " We pray sixty times in the day and fifty times in the night ", Pachomius said. In the Middle Ages the number of *Our Fathers* recited were counted on a string, and later the *Hail Marys*, in fact a hundred-and-fifty *Ave Marias* were substituted for the hundred-and-fifty Psalms which ordinary people did not know. The danger of mechanical recitation was realised, and that was why the fifteen decades of the Rosary were subordinated to the meditation on the fifteen mysteries from the life of Our Lady. We are given a glimpse of the life of prayer of a cultured lady at the end of the Middle Ages. St. Antoninus of Florence was her spiritual director, and he demanded a daily oral recitation of the seven penitential psalms, the litany of the Saints, the Little Office of the Cross with sixteen *Our Fathers*, the first nocturn and lauds of the Office of the Day, and, in addition, if possible, the Little Office of our Blessed Lady ; besides which of course morning and evening prayers and grace at meal-times.

Just as nuns and priests were bound to say their Office and recite the Breviary, so certain devout people set themselves a definite amount of prayers to recite every day. Prayer became an achievement which was offered to God every day, the culmination of St. Benedict's *Operi dei nihil praeponatur.*

The Salesian system is very different. As we have already said, St. Francis de Sales sees the highest task of man in giving his whole personality with all strength to God—" *Sans fin, sans mesure, sans reserve* " (Without end, without measure, without reserve). Thus he sees in prayer not only an act of homage to God, but values it quite specially in its ascetical meaning. Prayer is not conceived as the summit of personal achievement to which all else is subordinate, but as a means of increasing one's love of God, and also as an expression of this love which is the final goal of all religious striving. " God," he declares in the *Traitté*, " whose goodness exceeds all praise, does not gain through our praises—He neither becomes richer nor greater nor happier. But it is the essence of love to wish well to the beloved, and this urges us to praise God's endless goodness, and hence our prayer of praise is not only pleasing to God but something that corresponds to our nature and expresses the respectful love which we owe to Him." Of course the praying soul knows that " it can wish God no growth in goodness . . . it merely desires that His name should be always venerated and adored ". In a sermon of the year 1615 the saint said : " The goal of prayer is union with God. God does not need the prayer. Prayer is the transfiguration of the soul " . . .[1]

So in the Salesian system the *opus Dei* appears similarly an *opus animi*. Prayer serves to honour God, but also to render the soul holy. The difference of this conception from the Benedictine is expressed by Vincent when he says " the Salesian soul does not say ' All for the *Officium* —including becoming holy ' ; it says ' All for sancti- fication—including the *Officium* '. The *opus Dei* becomes merely a means ". Of course this does not mean St. Francis looks to the person before he looks to God. The Salesian idea, just as that of St. Benedict, and St. Thomas and other saints of the Middle Ages, puts God first, but

[1] *Œuvres*, Vol. VIII, p. 168.

this does not necessarily imply that the whole of religious life has to centre around liturgical prayer. The beginning and end of all religion—the adoration of God—are the same in the Mediæval as in the Salesian conception. But the idea of holiness in the Salesian system covers a greater field. It presents the whole person with all his potentialities. Augustine once said : " God seeks thee more than thy gifts ". Francis is imbued with this truth and hence he sees in prayer not only a gift to God but also a means of offering up our own selves.

The chief aim of prayer according to St. Francis is " the uniting of the soul with God ".[1] The union with God is achieved by love, and love is furthered rather by a free prayer from one's own soul than by the repetition catalogued by others. Consequently in the Salesian system the private prayer takes the first place, and the textual prayer the second.

This self-invented and private prayer is divided into two parts by Luis of Granada : " The first consists in the contemplation of all that which is calculated to make us love God . . . the second consists in beseeching God to inflame our hearts with love ". Both forms play a large part in Salesian piety, the first form giving rise to the second. When the first is there the second comes of itself. Hence the emphasis on contemplation plays a large part in Francis's system, though in his letters we see chiefly his yearning for love and his prayers beseeching God to give him more and more grace.

Now history shows that religious life based on inner prayer, and especially on contemplation, reached completion during the Sixteenth Century. The mediæval monastery was centred entirely around community

[1] *Œuvres*, Vol. VIII, p. 168.

prayer, and yet there was very little mention of methodical contemplation. At the end of the Fourteenth and Fifteenth Centuries there was a slow turn in this direction, first in the Netherlands and then in Spain. Ignatius, Luis of Granada and John of Avila gave detailed directions for contemplative prayer. St. Ignatius renounced choral prayer in favour of it, as also did St. Francis of Assisi. St. Francis de Sales goes further still and wants the congregation of the *Visitation* to lay stress " before everything else " on the holy and heartfelt " inner unity " with God. Therefore he recommends " an hour of inner prayer every morning and evening ". In the place of the Breviary prayers he places the Little Office of Our Lady with the observation that the sisters will thus have " a happy and holy recreation ".[1] Among the reasons which decided him to introduce the Little Office he mentions that " the Sisters have various spiritual practices which they could not have if they said the great Office ". Many contemporaries thought that an Order without the prayers of the Breviary was unheard of, and therefore attacked its system referring to the example of others. Francis, however, never wavered : " I hope that God will help us and that the greater Office will never be introduced into this congregation. The Pope himself has approved of this ". Of the people who gave him so much unsolicited advice he merely said, " One must be patient with people who are well-meaning ".[2]

It would be very wrong to think that Francis underestimated the value of Breviary prayer. On the contrary, Francis advised the introduction of the Tridentine Breviary into a convent which said the greater Office.

[1] *Œuvres*, Vol. XIV, pp. 306, 330.
[2] *Œuvres*, Vol. XIX, pp. 141, 203.

He desired a careful preparation for the Office through acts of contrition and prayers to the Holy Ghost, and demanded a correct observation of the Rubrics on Feast Days. He wanted even lay people to be present at Vespers on Sundays and week-days because the liturgy of the Church has a high value for increasing the love of God. Francis is a man of sympathies who does not set individual directions against each other with an " either —or " but rather reconciles them with " and—also ". But it is undeniable that his emphasis is primarily on inner prayer, just as the Benedictine emphasis is on the Choir Office.

This orientation to interior prayer has influenced Catholic life since his time and probably will influence it more still in the future. One order after another took up contemplation and meditation, first of all the Dominicans, and at last the Benedictines. In 1918 the Canon Law of the Church urged it as a duty. One can imagine that if the development continues the way it has begun, contemplation will play the same part in a priest's life as the Breviary.

Francis's emphasis on interior prayer is a little more obvious in his advice to the laity. Athanasius had said : Learn the Psalms, but Francis teaches his pupils to meditate. It is interesting to notice that in his youth he too shared the high esteem for textual prayer. Even at the age of twenty-seven he sent " formulæ of prayers " to crusaders. His change of emphasis probably occurred in the year 1602 during his sojourn in Paris when he studied the religious life closely. It was then that he made a short direction for contemplative prayer. It is certain that already in 1604 he gave various members of his flock a *petit memorial* that was concerned with meditative prayer, and in the *Introduction* he expounds his method of meditation in seven chapters.

Many people objected that the ordinary lay person was scarcely capable of meditation because the gift of inner prayer is rare enough. For example, Hugh of St. Victor says " that simple meditation was not for beginners but for those who have already advanced in spiritual life, while contemplation should be reserved for the third degree—the perfect ". The Spanish masters of the Sixteenth Century agreed with this, and Luis of Granada especially says that " Meditation is a thing for priests and monks, and not for people in the world ". Francis answered : " Everybody can attain this gift, even the rawest souls, if they only have a good director and are prepared to give themselves as much trouble as the thing deserves ".[1]

He who strives after perfection should dedicate " an hour a day " to contemplation. Oral prayer can recede. " If you only cultivate interior prayer and besides this say the *Our Father*, *Ave Maria* and *Credo*, you can be satisfied with that ", and " if our Lord calls you to interior prayer during oral prayer you would do well to enter into it ".[2] What the saint recommends to individual souls in letters, he preaches to everyone in the *Introduction* : " If you possess the gift of interior prayer you can always place this first, therefore do not worry if various obligations prevent you carrying out oral prayer. The Lord's prayer is enough to complete your meditation, and if possible the Ave Maria and the Apostle's Creed. If during oral prayer you feel your heart drawn to interior prayer, let your spirit peacefully pass into it and do not

[1] *Œuvres*, Vol. III, p. 364.
[2] *Œuvres*, Vol. XIV, pp. 8, 270.

worry because you have not completed your oral prayer,
for the interior prayer is more pleasing to God and more
useful to yourself. I except the ecclesiastical Office, if
you are bound to recite it ; for in this case it is the fulfilling of a duty . . . ".[1]

St. Thomas Aquinas laid the foundation for this outlook. " In private prayer one should use the voice and
other external manifestations only in so far as they serve
the interior awakening of the spirit. If the soul were in
some way distracted or hampered by it then it should be
discontinued." " Who behaves otherwise, *i.e.*, persists
in oral prayer even when incited to enter into interior
prayer, renounces the goal so as to retain the means to
the goal." The aim of prayer is the union of the soul
with God, and this is not helped by the greatness and
beauty of the ideas which we express but by the amount
of spiritual energy which we expend in thinking of these
ideas, turning them over and stating them afresh. It is
undeniable that even the most beautiful prayers cease to
hold our attention after a certain amount of time, and as
a consequence we are menaced by the danger of
mechanical repetition. Francis knew all this, and therefore he desired the most intensive activity from each
individual soul. Inner, self-created prayer by its very
nature demands greater application than the repetition
of a textual prayer, for as soon as our attention wanders
our prayer stops. The fact that one is tired after inner
contemplation shows that the use of energy and personal
strain is considerably greater in interior prayer than by
the repetition of formulæ, and Francis sees tiredness as a
" desirable indication " of good prayer.[2]

[1] *Œuvres*, Vol. III, p. 72.
[2] *Œuvres*, Vol. XVII, p. 9.

From his belief that the value of prayer depends upon the intensity with which the soul turns its forces to God, Francis judges the length of prayer. " If you are unable to pray attentively for half-an-hour then pray only a quarter of an hour, or only the half of a quarter of an hour." Of course the saint does not consider a prayer of half-an-hour to be long, but if the soul is incapable of such concentration then the prayer should be shortened to the measure of the capability, for a spiritless continuation would be a mere waste of time. Oral prayer, without meditation, is no more than a mere " lip-murmuring ", and has the same value before God as a parrot saying prayers.[1] " The quantity of everything must be measured by the end," said St. Thomas, and he drew the conclusion that the duration of the prayer should be determined by the spiritual power of concentration ; when this is exhausted the prayer should end. Francis is of the same opinion : " one *Our Father* has greater value if prayed with the whole soul than many *Our Fathers* carelessly repeated ". " Our progress does not rest on the length of our prayers but on the perfection with which we say them." Francis mentions the laughable consequences of the opposite view to his Nuns : " Last year you fasted three times a week . . . if you now want to double your fasts the whole week is covered. What will you do next year ? either you must lengthen the week to nine days, or have a fast day twice on the same day ".[2]

" *Courtement et fervemment* " (shortly but fervently) is his motto.[3] It may happen that one has scarcely any time for morning prayers and is dead-tired in the evening.

[1] *Œuvres*, Vol. XIV, p. 53.
[2] *Œuvres*, Vol. VI, pp. 109, 114.
[3] *Œuvres*, Vol. XVII, p. 167.

But one always has enough time to kneel down with a fervent and heartfelt glance to greet the Heavenly Father —" and if it be only for three minutes it should never be missed ". Francis lays a very special value on what we call ejaculatory prayer. This was not new, since Egyptian monachism knew it and St. Augustine refers to it. But the high value given it is new. Luis of Granada describes it as " the first and principal exercise " and states that it is " an effective means of making oneself perfect in love ". With St. Francis this estimation is even clearer. He speaks of it in his first letters of direction and devotes a whole chapter in the *Introduction* to it. " On this," he declares, " rests the great work of perfection. In case of necessity it can replace all other prayers, and if it is lacking nothing else can fill the gap . . . therefore in future take it to heart and never forget it." [1]

Francis describes the essence of ejaculatory prayer as a " short but fiery lifting of the heart to God ". By means of ejaculatory prayers the soul surrenders itself to God " a thousand times a day ". " It reaches up to Him like a child to its father." " *Divers mouvements* " (divers movements of the heart)—is Francis's definition of ejaculations. We must remember that movement is, according to Francis, the essence of love, and therefore ejaculatory prayers are acts of pure love, the pressing of the heart " to give itself up to the love of God and to inflame a tender love for the Heavenly Bridegroom ".

These acts of love can take the form of definite words. Verses of songs or sentences from the *Canticle of Canticles* may be used, but usually the soul will formulate its own expressions. In the *Directoire Spirituel* for the Order of the Visitation Francis gives a number of examples (they

[1] *Œuvres*, Vol. III, p. 100.

should be taken as examples only and not as established formulæ for all). " My view," he declares, " is this ; do not bind yourselves to definite words, but utter with your heart or your mouth what love dictates at the moment." Two examples that he mentions in a sermon—" I love You " and " My All "—show that they are momentary expressions of feeling. If we are anxious about anything in life, he urges the prayer : " On you, O Lord, I set my hope ". " Say it often," he continues in the letter, " Say it with glowing feeling, say it with boldness, and we will forthwith think : I will not be confounded." [1] Sometimes the soul needs no word whatsoever, " not even interior words are necessary ". " We speak with a glance alone," as spouses passing by greet one another with the eyes. The love which surges up in the heart is enough. " Love must be active." [2] It must always be thinking of the beloved, calling to him and rejoicing. Men of the world have hardly any idea what the love of God is, and that is why Francis refers to a love which they understand —" human and natural love ". Here they learn from earthly experience what love wants. " Lovers are nearly always thinking of each other. Their hearts are full of affection for each other, their mouths are filled with praise. In separation they lose no opportunity of showing their love by letters. They write the name of their beloved on the bark of every tree." So similarly people who love God cannot cease to think of Him. They breathe for Him and thirst after Him, and were it possible " they would like to engrave on the breasts of everyone in the world the holy and sublime name of Jesus ".[3]

---

[1] *Œuvres*, Vol. XXV, pp. 152–154.
[2] *Œuvres*, Vol. XIII, p. 150.
[3] *Œuvres*, Vol. III, pp. 95 *sq.*

This love is the source from which the ejaculatory prayer derives. The condition of love necessitates the unloading of the heart in acts of love, and wherever true devotion lies it will bring forth this fruit. The life of day to day is powerless to restrain it ; the loving soul will find a reason for thinking of the beloved everywhere. " All things invite you to this and every creature sings the praise of the beloved." It is certain that the Saint expected an incentive to the love of God to come from the contemplation of nature.

He seeks the way to God not in the contempt of the creature ; he does not flee from the world's reality, nor does he ever see that dualism which cleaves God from the world, nor hope to attain the heavenly through the rejection of the earthly. On the contrary, the visible world is for him a mirror of the Invisible God.

St. Francis of Assisi, St. Gertrude and St. Teresa hold the same view, and it approaches to the symbolical mediæval contemplation of nature whose founder was Hugh of St. Victor (died 1141). " The whole visible world," the latter declared, " is as a book written with God's finger. Individual creatures are like pictures traced by God so as to announce His wisdom." God equipped man with a double sense " so that he should survey the visible through the flesh and the invisible through the mind, so that the visible and invisible should inspire him to praise his Creator ". This conception of the world and this tendency of man to contemplate God's creation show us that it is God's will that man should love the world so as " to progress to love of the Creator through admiration of His creation ". Of course fools only admire the outer appearances, " but the wise man penetrates through what he sees to a deeper knowledge

of divine wisdom ". He " knows how to turn the beauty
of the physical world to spiritual use ". Beyond the
beauty of created things he strives upwards to the " beauty
which is more beautiful than any beauty . . . for it is
good always to contemplate and admire the works of
God ".

From this spiritual attitude a whole literature evolved
which explained nature as the symbol of religious ideas.
The universe reflects the thoughts of God. Vincentius
of Beauvais calls his great encyclopædia *The Great Mirror.*
Of Animals and Other Things is the title of a writing ascribed
to Hugh of St. Victor. These allegorical natural histories
were the sources from which preachers found the symbolism for their sermons, and artists the many pictures of
animals and plants which were copied in Gothic archi-
tecture. Often their meaning is no longer perceptible to
modern men.

We see Francis's use of natural history in a letter which
he wrote to the brother of Madame de Chantal in 1604.
This brother had risen from the subdiaconate to being
a bishop, and the letter consists of detailed advice as to
how to form a good sermon. He speaks of the various
sources of help. He asks : " And what about using
natural histories ? " (The very plural shows the amount
of literature that had been written on the subject.)
" Very well," continues the saint, " because the world
was created through God's word, it bears in every part
traces of this word. All its parts sing the praise of the
Master. It is a book that contains God's word, but in a
language not understood by everyone. But anyone who
has learnt to understand it through meditation, does very
well to make use of it. Thus did St. Anthony (the hermit)
who possessed no other library . . . ' The heavens relate

the glory of God '. Nature is good for similes and comparisons and for a thousand other things." [1] Francis's own sermons, his letters, the *Introduction*, and the *Traitté* show that he enthusiastically followed the method he recommended. It is true that he seldom gives examples which rest on his own observation of nature. Much more frequently he quotes out of books, following the fashion of his time. And his chief source is the elder Pliny, who ravished every educated humanist, and the mediæval natural histories already mentioned.

Let us add here his words written in the *Introduction* at the end of his discussion on ejaculatory prayer. " Unhappy are they who separate the Creator from His creation, and turn to sin. But happy are they who relate creation to the magnificence of the Creator, and convert their vanity to the honour of truth." Thus we must recognise that the conceptions of Francis and Hugh are very similar. It is an open question whether the saint had actually read Hugh's writing, had become acquainted with them through other books, or had come to such similar conclusions by his own reflection.

It is certain that Francis knew Scupoli's *Spiritual Struggle*. The latter in his twenty-first chapter gives a clear instruction as to how to attain religious thoughts and feelings from the contemplation of nature, and to express them in the form of little ejaculatory prayers. " If you feel allured by the beauty of creatures, separate that which you see from the divine Spirit which you do not see but consider that all beauty that appears outwardly derives alone from that invisible Spirit." " If you notice splendid attributes to a thing, let your thoughts lead the creature back to its nothingness and fasten the

[1] *Œuvres*, Vol. XII, p. 307.

eye of your spirit on the high Creator. And taking joy in Him alone, say : O highest and most desirable One, how overjoyed am I that Thou alone art the eternal cause of every created thing." It is very probable that these words of Scupoli encouraged Francis to say what he did in the *Introduction*. Encouraged him, but did not inspire him—because what Francis writes is never a repetition of the thoughts of others but the outcome of his personal conviction. We only need to consider the difference between both conceptions. Scupoli approaches nature with the preconceived desire to reject quickly the earthly things through logical analysis, so as to advance to religion through abstraction and sublimation. The appearances of the exterior world are only the object from which thoughts rebound so as to mount upwards to God. With Francis we find, as usual, the attitude of affirmation. He takes an unrestrained joy in creatures and he tarries lovingly with them, but deep love weaves its own thoughts round every picture that the eyes see. For this he needs no method of " separating and contrasting ", as Scupoli expresses it, no logical processes of thought. His love cannot do otherwise than think of that for which all its meditation and aspiration exists—always and everywhere. Luis of Granada expressed this finely : " He who really loves God sees Him in all things : all things appear to invite him to the love of God ". And St. Francis says that the Salesian soul achieves " good thoughts and holy yearnings from all things that the diversity of this mortal life offers to the eyes ". With St. Gregory Nazianzen the soul can proclaim : " I have become accustomed to use all things in my spiritual progress ".

Francis's contemporary, the famous Cardinal Robert Bellarmine, set down the religious contemplation of nature in a monograph a few years after the publication of the *Introduction, Concerning the ascent of the soul to God by the ladder of created things*. In it he writes : " O my soul, whatever wonderful thing thou seest may it be to thee a rung in the ladder that leads to the knowledge of the perfection of the Creator ; of Him Who is incomparably greater and more wonderful than all created things ". He considers : " No other ladder that leads to God appears so accessible to us mortals as that which mounts by means of the creations of God ". Francis knew and treasured the book. Because Bellarmine had written it in his old age, Francis, in a letter to him, called it " that last-born and dearest Benjamin ". Bellarmine's method comes near to that of his compatriot Scupoli. Francis de Sales' conception lies somewhere between this method and the all-animating nature-love of St. Francis of Assisi.

But now we ask : how is it possible to educate the soul to such an activity of love that all earthly experience will become for it an urge towards the love of God ? First let us ask the contrary question : Is it possible to strengthen the activity of a habitus without operating on the habitus itself ? Can one acquire fruit without the detour of nursing the fruit-tree ? The effort could, of course, be made. An ejaculatory prayer could be said so many times a day. Francis too declares at first it is a " useful exercise to say ejaculations every time the hour strikes ". But he gives this advice as early as 1604, at the beginning of his activity as a director. Later he warns us against making it a duty to " carry out a definite number of genuflections, ejaculatory prayers, or similar practices daily ".[1] He does not like numerical estimates. He

[1] *Œuvres*, Vol. XII, p. 358.

himself speaks quite generally of a " dozen " or of " a thousandth time ". He fears anything mechanical, and experience has proved the rightness of this fear. The real spontaneity of love cannot be induced by a mechanical system of ejaculations when the clock strikes, and any effort to excite spiritual fervour through regimentation tends to be from outside inwards, whereas Francis pursues the opposite method. A concentration on the strike of the clock is definitely an outside-inwards way of leading a soul to God. The activity of love must first be interior, and it is only if ejaculatory prayers are pure acts of love that they have any value. Only as acts of love are they able to give strength to the habitus.

Love is the essence of perfection, and it must be furthered by the natural laws which God has placed in the soul. The education of the apprehension is only possible by way of experience. Contemplation continuously creates and cultivates the basis in binding the understanding, will and affections to the highest good. For it is in acts of love that the habitus of love is fostered : in them man experiences his love, and from the reflex action of this experience the habitus itself receives fresh impetus. The fact strengthens the ability.

(v) THE LAW OF LOVE

Asceticism of love—that is Francis's method. Out of this derives a further observation which we make in studying his writings, that the saint does not lay as great a value on exterior guarantees as do other spiritual directors.

It is a well-known fact that young people—and equally beginners in religious life—set themselves a programme of life.   Because one knows that one's character is not yet formed, one creates for oneself a perfect type of finished man so as to have a detailed ideal of behaviour to live up to.   One draws up a careful rule of life, the reason of which is the sense of one's own uncertainty.   One is not quite sure of oneself : one fears one's weakness, and the binding of oneself assures the future.   Thus the bonds are tied more tightly, the weaker and more unsure one feels.

In later years the programme is usually wrecked by experience.   The chief reason for this does not lie in personal weakness, but in the programme itself.   It did not sufficiently take into account either personal peculiarities or particular events in life's reality, for at the time when the rule was drawn up little was known of the world and still less of the self.   The programme should have been a help in the march forward, but when this help does not carry out what it promised it becomes a burden, and a limitation to freedom of movement.   One lays it aside and observes it against the background of moral effort generally, subsequently renouncing such progress as is known to be unrealisable.   A sad, but unfortunately not a rare, result of noble beginnings.

St. Francis de Sales was fully aware of this.   He does not speak of it, but his advice shows that he has observed this phenomenon closely and examined its psychological background carefully.   He does not believe that such programmes are an assurance of the future.   He wants practical resolutions, from which the deed is sure to follow ;   he does not want a theoretical rule which orders one's life down to the smallest detail and for years to come.   Only the basic direction of the will to love God

should be tightly anchored. We should say every day
with David : " Now I begin to love my God very much ".
We ought never to forget this axiom of the saint's, that it
is good " always again to begin anew ", to progress
" step by step ", and " from one stage to another ".
Francis declares : " It is very good to strive with a
universal longing for the highest perfection of Christian
life : but one should not philosophise over details ".
That can be useful only if it happens " from day to day
according to day-to-day happenings ". [1]

Francis's literary remains show us the realisation of this
theory in the practical direction of souls. Consider, for
example, the act of consecration with which the soul
begins its new life in God. Francis provides a text for this
in the *Introduction*. There he says : " I bind myself
irrevocably to serve God, and to love Him now and always.
With this object I dedicate, give, and consecrate to Him
my soul with all its capabilities, my mind with all its
powers, my heart with all its affection, and my body with
all its senses ". The totality of the dedication reaches
complete expression. There is no mention of the means
of realising it though Francis gives penetrating directions
about this later. He wants an ordering of the individual
day and the individual year. He knows well that life is
built up on details. But these details should not be
formed into a rigid rule whose realisation is a duty and
whose transgression is sin. He tells the daughters of the
Visitation, that the rules of the order " are binding neither
under mortal nor under venial sin ".[2]

This is not only for beginners. Those who have made
progress, too, should preserve their freedom of action in

---

[1] *Œuvres*, Vol. XIII, p. 19 ; Vol. XIV, p. 22 ; Vol. XVI, p. 311.
[2] *Œuvres*, Vol. III, p. 60 ; Vol. VI, p. 12.

daily life. Francis forbids his nuns to bind themselves
" to a definite number of prayers and similar practices ".
At least such a decision must be preceded by a discussion
with the superior, even if the obligation is only to be valid
for " a certain time ". Similarly he advises against the
turning of a good intention into an imperative " must ",
because " it is necessary that a holy freedom and liberty
should reign, and that we should be under no law or
obligation other than that of love ".[1] Francis demands
attention to this holy freedom from teachers especially.
" Do not make our little Aymée," he wrote to Madame
de Chantal, " so good that she despises us." [2] " Despise "
is a strong expression, but it shows a deep understanding
of the youthful soul. As spiritual director Francis is
always emphasising that his directions are always to be
understood " *grosso modo* ". Moreover, he describes this
" large scale " writing as the " general rule " for the
interpretation of all his letters. He declares that he is
giving advice but not commands. " The only thing that
advice requires is that it should not be scorned . . . it is
in no way binding." [3] Madame de Chantal, who had
been held in the closest subjection by her earlier confessor,
besought him for a vow of obedience. Francis replied :
" I am leaving you the spirit of freedom . . . If you love
subjection and obedience very much, then I would advise
you on certain occasions to omit your exercises—consider
this as a sort of obedience—and make up for the lack
through love ". " Do not be troubled if you do not do
something that I have ordered. For the general rule of
our obedience is—I am writing it in capital letters—

[1] *Œuvres*, Vol. VI, p. 167 ; Vol. XIII, p. 184.
[2] *Œuvres*, Vol. XIII, p. 365.
[3] *Œuvres*, Vol. XII, p. 359 ; Vol. XIII, p. 374.

ONE MUST DO ALL OUT OF LOVE AND NOTHING FROM COMPULSION. One must love obedience more than fear disobedience." [1]

From this background Francis makes war on every overcharging of the soul with measures for improving it. He rejects " such an exact rule " for cloister life. He counsels the nunneries not to place themselves under the monasteries of the same rule, because though these latter are magnificent servants of God " they nevertheless have the habit of taking away from women the holy freedom of the spirit ". He declines every exaggeration of authority—" a great error "—whether in theory or in practice. " This was his maxim," Camus informs us, " this was the spirit of the whole of his government : All through love and nothing through force. He often said to me : Those who force people's wills are practising a tyranny abhorrent to God and man. For this reason he could not agree with those tyrannous souls who demanded obedience, whether it is given willingly or unwillingly. When I complained to our blessed father concerning the opposition against a certain good thing that I wanted to carry out, he said to me : You have the spirit of tyranny. . . . Do you want to do more than God and force the will of creatures whom God created with free will ? You act peremptorily in this question as though the wills of your diocesans were entirely in your hands. And God, Who has all hearts in His, does not do this." So Francis wanted one to " conduct oneself . . . in the spiritual leadership of souls as God would, namely, to inspire, comfort, enlighten, admonish, beseech, and yet behave with all patience. One should knock at the door of the heart like a bridegroom, so that it will be

[1] *Œuvres*, Vol. XII, p. 359.

opened with love. One should usher in salvation with joy, and if it is refused, endure the refusal with love ".

Francis preserves an extraordinary reserve, though he, as a religious and educational genius, had more right than anyone else to play a part in ordering other people's lives. We must freely admit that it was only because he held the reins with such a genial hand that he was able to attain the desired goal. Average people incline instinctively to the easier method of force, and of course Francis himself knew how to apply the Church's sanctions in cases of flagrant insubordination. " I want absolute obedience," he declared in an important matter, and on another occasion he gave his command under threat of excommunication, *sub poena excommunicationis latae sententiae*.[1] But these few examples lie in questions of exterior law. They serve the accomplishment of the Kingdom of God in this world. In the realm of the interior life he always appeals to love. And he says quite explicitly to his disciples : " I leave you the spirit of freedom ". " All through love, and nothing through force."

Let us look for a moment at Ignatius. In the constitution of his order he writes : " All who live under obedience should be aware that . . . they must let themselves be moved and ruled by their superiors, as though they were a corpse which can be moved everywhere and be treated in any way ". This might seem a very great contrast, but actually Francis too expected his directions to be carried out exactly, and the practical outcome of both methods of direction is not so very different. The difference is mainly verbal. Ignatius, the soldier, is accustomed to the tone of command, whereas Francis, the polite nobleman, lives in circles in which

[1] *Œuvres*, Vol. XII, p. 186 ; Vol. XVIII, p. 2.

one says please. " You must," commands Ignatius.
" Could you not ? " Francis asks, and is convinced that
what he asks will be done. His method could be characterised : I, no, I do not command, but you know what
you ought to do. Ignatius uses authority. Francis turns
to the conscience of those under his control, to the inner
law of the love of God which is written in the heart through
grace.

The essential difference between the methods of the
two saints is based in their different conception of the
relationship between God and man, to which we have
already referred. With Ignatius the majesty of God, our
King and Lord, stands in the foreground. Unconditional
obedience naturally results from that. Hence Ignatius
commands. Francis places love in the centre. The
initiative lies with love. It suffices to awaken it, hold it
on high, and point out the way to it. Hence Francis
gives advice. This advice " does not bind, but requires
that one should not despise it ". This moral requirement
to think over the counsel given, and apply it to one's own
life, is clearly emphasised by Francis. Doubtless there
will occur particular occasions " which make it appear
right and desirable " to behave in another way. Francis
admits it ; but says that the desirability of the different
behaviour must be judged by reason enlightened by faith
and not by caprice. What Francis admits and recommends is nothing else but what theology since Albert the
Great calls *Epikeia*. One abandons the way pointed out
by the command or counsel, not because it is more
comfortable but because it is better : not because one
prefers one's own judgment to authority, but in the
conviction that the authority itself, in the exceptional
case before one, would decide in this way. " I want you

to consider this as a kind of obedience," declares Francis. He presumes that the soul " loves obedience very much ".

Man is bound to the law of God and to the law of His representatives in the world and the Church. This obligation seems like an " iron chain " if one only follows it when forced by fear. It shines like a " golden chain " when one's love of God, the Lawgiver, brings one also to love His commandment. So Christ's word is realised : " My yoke is sweet and my burden light ". " On the royal galleon of the love of God there are no galley slaves, but only voluntary rowers," declares Francis, according to the statement of Camus. In his direction of souls Francis lays hold not of iron but of golden chains. He has confidence in the force of love. " The love of Christ forces us," wrote the Apostle of the Gentiles. To what ? To the fulfilling of all justice, to the observation of the commandments, to the following of the appropriate advice. The " devotion of this highly-developed love decides us to do the good, as far as we know, even when it is not commanded, but only directed by a counsel and a suggestion ".[1]

Francis always wants the soul to have room to expand and to possess the joyous feeling of freedom of movement. He is in no sense a follower of anyone who expects perfection to come from a narrowing-down of movement ; and the Catholic tradition of education justifies him. Isidor of Seville (died 636) demands that a reasonable legislation should limit itself to the necessary. The mediæval theologians underline this sentence with penetrating arguments. St. Thomas especially demands wise moderation. The lawgiver does not need to forbid

[1] *Œuvres*, Vol. III, pp. 15 *sq.*

everything that a virtuous man refrains from doing any-way, but should only command what is necessary. Otherwise he is in danger of producing the opposite of what he intends. "The more laws, the more thieves," said Lao-Tse two thousand five hundred years ago. Francis demands the same wisdom for the small circle of a monastery, for the formation of the individual person-ality. St. Thomas had already exposed the principle. "Well-intentioned people," he says, "are more easily brought to virtue when one turns to exhortation of their free will than when one employs force." The moral progress is in any case greater when the pupil does good freely because of guidance and encouragement than when he only does it when forced through a command.

In brief, St. Francis de Sales does not expect perfection from a prescription from outside the soul, whether imposed by another or by one's own will. He rather wants the concordance with the will of God to become an interior law of the personality, a peculiarity of the soul.

What he strives after is precisely a realisation of what the Holy Scripture announces as the essence of the New Testament law. Paul compares this with the judaic and worldly law as "the law of belief", of "grace", "the law of the spirit" which frees us inwardly from sin. John describes it as "the word of God that remains in you" that "teaches you all things", through which "you are strong . . . and have overcome evil". The Fathers of the Church, like Irenæus and Chrysostom, develop this doctrine further : Augustine speaks of a new law that God wrote in our hearts. "The law of God written in the heart is nothing else than the presence of the Holy Ghost . . . which is the fulfilling of the law." "To have written the law of God in our hearts means to embrace with most reverent affection the justice of the law." Thomas constructs the inheritance of tradition into the system of moral theology. " The essence of the new law is the grace of the Holy Ghost, which proclaims itself in the belief which becomes effective through love."

Belief shows the way to God ; love gives the driving force to turn to him. Thus the New Testament law is an inner law which comprehends the depth of the soul. In it lies a certain similarity with the natural moral law which already exists in men : except that this has its roots in human nature, while the New Testament law is inculcated through the Holy Ghost. So the new law appears as the " perfect law of freedom ". Man now wants what God wills. This likeness is made effective through love. Hence it is called " the fulfilment of the law ". Augustine shows us the result of this inner harmony of the perfect Christian with the will of God when he says : " Love and do what you will ".

This old teaching of the Church which, it must be admitted, is too little emphasised by many theologians, is what St. Francis de Sales brings to full flowering in his Ascetic. For him the *essential* is not the external cabining of the will by what is forbidden under pain of sin. Small souls may be satisfied with the rare laurels of such a result, but Francis, the genius and the saint, sees further. He wants to change man interiorly and form him to the likeness of God. This transformation is the work of the Holy Ghost, the pneumatical " anointment " of which St. John speaks. Man can only do one thing for it : love God with his whole heart and his whole strength. That is the essential thing.

The psychology of love determines the way of asceticism. Love rules over all the inclinations of the heart. Love

alone breaks up the yearning for forbidden things : for
" what does one desire if one does not love it ? " " How
happy is the interior Kingdom when it is ruled by holy
love ! " " How blessed are all the forces of our soul when
they obey a King so holy and so wise." " No, . . . where
one obeys Him, in His Kingdom, He never allows great
sins of any sort to dwell, not even an attachment to the
smallest." The sins exist only here in this world, " so as
to practise the interior virtue in struggle, and make it
courageous ".[1]

(vi) LOVE AND DANGER

Thus the basic idea of Salesian asceticism is to push
holy love forward to flaming enthusiasm : then the white
heat of love of God will dissolve the red heat of sinful lust.
Let us conform human desire with God's will, and it no
longer needs a strong rein. In free action then, one
behaves as prescription and law command. That is the
meaning of the words of St. Peter : " Be subject . . . as
free : not as those who use freedom to cover up evil, but
as servants of God ". It must be admitted that no man
is capable of attaining an uninterrupted harmony between
his own will and the will of God. That would be sinlessness, and it was only realised in Christ and Mary. But
the common share of all religious people should be the
affirmation of this perfection in one's feelings and the
education of one's " I " to a pure mirror of divine
holiness.

If the soul has achieved this basic position it possesses
that highest love of God which dedicates itself unreservedly
to the eternal. But there is a possibility that some

[1] *Œuvres*, Vol. IV, p. 32 ; Vol. XIII, pp. 383 *sq.*

external incitement to sin may suddenly overturn this state of love, and with this knowledge we have found the key to the last consequence of Salesian asceticism : the way through the world should involve no foolhardy risk for a well-formed person.

If the soul is tightly anchored in God, then Francis has no fears of the storms of life. Of course the saint knew the dangers of the world at least as well as other ascetical teachers. But this did not prompt him to accept the watchword : Shun and flee, though Tertullian preached " Fear is the basis of salvation " and though the inheritors of his maxim demanded flight from life for holy people. Francis's preference goes—he uses this comparison—not to those clever animals which smell out every danger, and then, when confronted with it, withdraw—like the fox, for example—but to the " lion, which is a very noble animal. The lion trusts in his boldness and, in the simplicity of its heart, sleeps as readily in the middle of a thoroughfare as in a withdrawn nook ". " Where no danger of mortal sin threatens, one must not flee, but be victorious over all enemies. We must obstinately withstand our enemies, not losing courage even if we are conquered by them once or twice." [1]

Moral theology calls all incitement to evil which comes upon us from outside occasions of sin. And it establishes that it is our duty to flee " the proximate occasion of serious sin ", i.e., all those occasions through which, if frequented, a serious sin can be foreseen as probable. But this does not mean that one should walk in fear and trepidation, seeking all the small dangers, because that would mean that " numberless useful actions would remain undone through fear of sin ". Such an attitude

[1] Œuvres, Vol. VI, p. 220 ; Vol. XIV, p. 29.

could never be held by a man of foresight, but by a coward. Francis is of the same opinion. " One ought not to be so timorous that one leaves the good and the right undone . . . nor so presumptuous and foolhardy as to walk into danger and remain in it, without being prepared to stand by one's duties." [1]

Let us take an example to prove it. The saint knew the superficial life in the courts of princes. He had been in Paris, and in Annecy itself there was the Duke of Savoy. He cultivated friendly relations with religious persons whose position took them to the court. Augustine had protested that he would never recommend anyone to live at court. Francis quotes him and refers to the " dictum of the wise men : He who wishes to live piously, let him flee the court and leave the palace ".[2] He describes himself as a " sworn enemy of courts ", and declares : " I have no especially good opinion of the court, and I think that one serves God better far from the court than in it ".[3] But for all that, over M. de Charmoysi, the husband of the historical *Philothea*, he delivers the judgment : His " virtue is so established that it will not be overturned by this wind ". He hopes that the Duc de Bellegarde, like the famous fire-flies of Pliny, will " tarry in the midst of the flame, without burning his wings ".[4] Moreover, when the fifteen-year-old son of Madame de Chantal was going out " on to the high sea of the world " by going to court, he wrote him a letter full of wishes of blessing and fatherly advice. He begins by saying : " I am not so timorous as many others. I do not consider this position as something mortally dangerous for a well-

---

[1] *Œuvres*, Vol. V, p. 327.
[2] *Œuvres*, Vol. XIV, p. 184.
[3] *Œuvres*, Vol. XIV, pp. 176, 184.
[4] *Œuvres*, Vol. XVI, p. 213.

formed soul and a manly courage, for Elizabeth of
Hungary became a saint in the midst of court-life. She
often played and danced without harming her holiness :
for this was so well rooted in her soul . . . that she
became greater in the midst of that pomp and vanity, in
which her position in life placed her ".[1] " How often do
we see people who grow holy in robes of silk and satin,
in cloaks and golden fabrics ? St. Radegond, the queen
of France, St. Elizabeth, the queen of Hungary, St.
Elizabeth, queen of Portugal, and many others bear
witness to it." [2] " He who is not a slave of the court can
reverence the Lord of the court, and serve Him in
holiness." It is quite certain that " in all places one can
achieve a very high grade of perfection, if only one will ".
" I know very well," he protests, " one can live well in all
occupations in the world just as in religious orders." [3]

Thus Francis makes no effort to withdraw the souls
entrusted to him from court life or from the dangers of
the world. He does not represent the viewpoint that
flight is always healthier for religious development than
fight. War and victory, too, have their formative value.
" Rest which is not tested in storm, is a lazy and deceitful
rest." " True virtue is not nourished in external rest."
He is convinced that the greater the external danger, the
greater the interior support of God : with the one
proviso that we always go into danger only according to
God's will. " God loves the souls moved by the waves
and storms of the world." [4]

If we look at the writings of the saint on the attitude
to be taken to friendship, good-fellowship, recreation,

[1] Œuvres, Vol. III, p. 253 ; Vol. XIV, p. 376.
[2] Œuvres, Vol. IX, p. 205.
[3] Œuvres, Vol. XVI, p. 223.
[4] Œuvres, Vol. XIV, pp. 339, 365 ; Vol. XV, pp. 269 sq.

playing, and dancing, we find this outlook confirmed.
" *Je ne suis pas si peureux que plusieurs autres.*" (I am not so
timorous as some others.) " One must not flee from, but
conquer, all enemies."

But let us remember that Francis wrote different things
in different cases. For example, he wants every danger
to be held far from children. " Take care," he writes to
Madame de Chantal, " that the children sleep alone, not
only because of the young boy but also because of his
sisters. . . . Experience makes me think it advisable to
say this." Similarly he emphasises that " places where
there are vipers and basilisks " are no residence for
" tender souls ". For them " a change of air is necessary "
if they are to become healthy.[1] But the method of Port-
Royal which tried to exclude people altogether from the
world, which suspected even a walk in the open air as an
occasion of sin and endeavoured to hold its pupils in
prison as in a " cage " whose " opening " should be " well
closed "—this method of upbringing is in direct contradiction to Francis's view.

The object of education is to foster an internal determination which is ready to stand up to average dangers.
Therefore Francis sees the pedagogic of " do not look "
and " do not touch ", and " shield yourself and flee "
merely as a measure to be taken in certain circumstances
by very weak natures. His ideal is not external preservation but the inner security which grows out of a conscious
and loving union with God. No, closing oneself against
external influences is not enough. The soul must become
immune against the poison. And this immunity to evil
is provided only by the inner, enthusiastic love of God
which Francis calls Devotion. " If our Aymée wants to

[1] *Œuvres*, Vol. XII, p. 360 ; Vol. XIV, p. 205.

remain in the storm and blizzard of the world then
without doubt she must be fortified with a hundred-fold
more care in true virtue and piety." [1]

With these considerations behind him Francis de Sales
allows his disciples to journey out " on the high sea of
life ".   For that reason he does not arm the ship with
inflexible programmes and narrow prescriptions.   But the
motors of the ship are perfected in the measure that its
own velocity is shifted to every surge.

Love is the driving force of life.   To it goes Francis's
main interest in spiritual direction, to it his personal
striving.   For this he supplicates God unceasingly, for
himself and for those under his charge.   " O eternal Love,
my heart seeks Thee eternally.   Ah come Holy Ghost,
and fill our hearts with Thy love." [2]

" Love, love, O holy love, come and possess our
hearts." [3]

[1] Œuvres, Vol. XIII, p. 209.
[2] Œuvres, Vol. V, p. 346.
[3] Œuvres, Vol. XV, p. 73.

ENVOI

On the soft waves of the little lake of Anneçy the steamer goes—past the defiant ducal castle with its mediæval towers, over to Talloire, where beyond the foothills the high Alpine peaks appear. There, half-way up, the saint once stood and looked across the blue lake to the green banks opposite. He hoped for a restful old age here, sanctifying his own soul, and writing.

In an hour or two the railway takes us from the loveliness of the landscape to the heavy greatness of the high vale of Chamonix. The neck is tired with looking up at Mont Blanc, Europe's highest peak.

"If you want to understand the poet completely, you must go into the poet's land." This wealth of landscape which St. Francis surveyed can serve as symbol for the fulness of his spirit. Loving and tender, the basic tones caress the sensitive heart. Majestic greatness and salient heights force the understanding to homage, and an enthusiastic assent to the heights flows from his writing.

Francis was the director of many religious persons during his earthly life. He has been our director, too, in these hours in which we have sought to trace the religious and moral ideal in his writings. But he himself did not consider his direction and friendship as something that was limited to his earthly life. He declared in a letter that in the world beyond he would think of everyone who had been under his direction in this life. "When this earthly life is over, I will always make a simple request

to God's eternal goodness, that He fills your heart with His perfect love." [1] May his hand lead us, too, both in the study of his doctrine and in its realisation in life. Our whole life should obey the injunction which on Christmas Day, 1622, in his last letter,[2] he once again noted down :
" Love in God and for God."

[1] *Œuvres*, Vol. XV, p. 283.
[2] *Œuvres*, Vol. XX, p. 399.